A Penguin Special
There's Gold in Them Thar Pills

Alan Arnold Klass, B.A., M.D., F.R.C.S. Edinburgh, F.R.C.S. Canada, L.L.D., was born in Russia in 1907 and emigrated to Canada in 1913. He received his medical training in Winnipeg and postgraduate surgical training in London and Edinburgh. As an associate professor, he has taught in the Departments of Anatomy and Surgery at the University of Manitoba where he has also served on the Senate and Board of Governors. During the Second World War he served as a surgical specialist in the Canadian Army.

Active in many medical and non-medical societies, he was Chairman of the Medical Advisory Board, Cancer Institute and President of the College of Physicians and Surgeons in the Province of Manitoba. He was also Chairman of the Canadian Institute of International Affairs. In 1971 he was appointed Chairman of a special commission for the Government of Manitoba to study the manufacture and distribution of pharmaceutical drugs. Many of the recommendations have been incorporated in an advanced pharmaceutical programme for the province.

He has written extensively on the legal, moral and ethical aspects of professionalism, including *What is a Profession?* and *Professional Integrity and the State*, with particular emphasis on his concern for the relationship between a profession and the society which it serves. He has also published original research in the fields of cancer therapy and the surgery of abdominal blood vessels. Dr Klass is married, and lives in Winnipeg, where he maintains his practice as a consultant.

Alan Klass

There's Gold in
Them Thar Pills

An Inquiry into the
Medical-industrial Complex

Penguin Books

648396

Penguin Books Ltd,
Harmondsworth, Middlesex, England
Penguin Books Inc.,
7110 Ambassador Road, Baltimore, Maryland 21207, U.S.A.
Penguin Books Australia Ltd,
Ringwood, Victoria, Australia
Penguin Books Canada Ltd,
41 Steelcase Road West, Markham, Ontario, Canada
Penguin Books (N.Z.) Ltd,
182–190 Wairau Road, Auckland 10, New Zealand

First published 1975
Copyright © Alan Klass, 1975

Made and printed in Great Britain by
Hazell Watson & Viney Ltd,
Aylesbury, Bucks.

To Helen

Contents

Preface

Ever since earliest times the health of the public depended upon interactions that evolved between three major areas: the maker of drugs, the healer or prescriber, and a controlling authority. Through the years these principals have exerted effects upon patients, often beneficial, sometimes harmful, occasionally lethal.

From the beginning of the twentieth century makers of drugs became the modern drug industry; research-orientated, multinational in spread and influence, held in high esteem, and financially successful. With the rare exception of the individual who lives a healthy life, without ever requiring medical care, and then suddenly drops dead, all of us trust our lives to the integrity of these three principals, but especially to the drug maker. The theme of this book is how the drug industry has replaced the doctor as the central agent in our system of health delivery.

The growth of the scientific education of the medical profession has occurred concurrently with the rise of the drug industry. The same burst of scientific knowledge that revolutionized drug production created rapid and continuing change in the knowledge and equipment of the doctor. Because of these parallel growths and because of modern industrial goals, the relative positions in the health system of drug-making on the one hand and doctoring on the other altered profoundly. While the doctor's reputation still stands high, his overall effect on public health is increasingly subject to critical questioning. Above all, the profession's relation to the drug industry has created a fundamental shift in their respective influences on public health.

When it became important to distinguish between a poison and a medication, government intervention for the control of the manufacture and the distribution of drugs became essential. If manufacture is careless, if storage is uncontrolled, if distribution is unrestricted and if dosage is unrestrained even the most harmless drug can be dangerous. All these matters of public safety must properly rest within the function of government.

In each of these three areas, professional, industrial and governmental, it is the public welfare that is at risk. How well each of these areas function in the interest of public health is also a matter of primary importance.

It is not intended to make this a statement that will answer all questions and explain economic theories, nor to quote the mathematical statistics of the drug industry. Much excellent material already written on this subject has relied upon figures in order to advance a particular argument. Sometimes, by the time the point is made, the thrust of the argument is lost in the deluge of economic theories and conflicting statistical evidence.

Travel through the streets of Calcutta and you will see poverty such as you have never seen. Should you accept this vision as evidence, sooner or later someone will demand statistical proof. What, for instance, is the per capita yearly earning expressed as purchasing power in Calcutta compared with the purchasing power of the native in Irkutsk? Before long the proof you have seen with your own eyes becomes dim and covered by a hazy film of irreconcilable numbers.

For most of my lifetime I have been actively engaged in the practice of medicine, particularly in the speciality of surgery. I have been involved in the 'care of the ill', on a person to person basis. I believe I know something of the trials and the misery that illness can bring to anyone, rich as well as poor. I have seen the wealthy beggared and the poor destroyed. I have also observed the growing dependence upon drugs in all levels of society and, in particular, the increasing reliance upon mood-elevating drugs for the depressed, as well as the enormous consumption of sedative drugs for the tense. I have witnessed and sometimes I have been a cooperator in the efforts of the drug industry to sell more and more of their profitable produce. I have seen the industry succeed. The industry succeeds because of its special kind of directed research, because of its highly efficient methods of production, but mainly because of its sophisticated promotion and marketing. I am convinced that its success derives from the fact, not recognized by doctors, that the drug industry has made captive my profession, the profession of medicine.

I have borne witness to this take-over by the drug industry from several points of view: as a practitioner in the field, from an involvement in professional matters, as a member of several professional associations, as a university teacher, and as a concerned citizen. This is an account of what I have seen, and of the events that I believe have diminished an honourable profession to the level of junior partner in an immensely powerful industrial-medical complex.

Acknowledgements

The author is grateful to Oxford University Press for permission to use extracts from *A History of the Royal College of Physicians of London*, Volume 1, 1964, Sir George Clark © Oxford University Press

Part 1

The Health System and the Public

1   The Beginning: Doctors, Poisons and Quacks

As long as man has existed poisons have been known, respected, treated with awe, with religious fervour, with malicious intent, and sometimes with honest attempts to heal. The earliest histories of both crime and medicine have much in common. Each has a story of witches' brews, extracts of known lethal agents, diluted hopefully with counteracting ingredients. The early history of the healing art is full of instructions on how to mix varying ingredients, many undoubtedly poisonous, in an honest, conscientious attempt to cure the ill by counteracting the malignant vapours or essences thought to have settled within the human frame.

In a superb history of the origins of the medical profession in England (*A History of the Royal College of Physicians of London*) Sir George Clark said:

Throughout the history of the world, those who seek wealth, or power, or reputation, or other desirable ends, by means which are generally regarded as proper and permissible, have had to contend against competitors who take shortcuts and disregard the accepted rules. Imposters infest every royal court, every political assembly, every enviable social circle, and every financial centre; they even penetrate into churches, armies, courts of justice, universities and learned societies. Nowhere have they persisted more incorrigibly than in the healing arts. The history of the warfare of the physician against the quacks is not a story with a plot, a story of strategies, defeats and victories leading on to a peace settlement; it is an interminable succession of incidents in which half of human nature collides with another.

Earliest attempts to distinguish between the good and the bad uses of the drugs led to legislation restricting their use to certain individuals deemed to be competent. In 1423 the College of Physicians of London came into being and about one hundred years later the granting of a Royal Charter by Henry VIII gave complete control to the College over the safety and use of drugs. Methods of control were crude but final. Certain members of the College called 'assessors' had the absolute right to enter any apothecary shop and, upon any evidence they themselves considered appropriate, were given the right to throw out into the street whatever they considered unfit, deleterious or impure. The basis for their judgement remains obscure and by modern scientific criteria without foundation. But, lest we become too smug with reference to scientific data, let us recall that the thalidomide tragedy occurred in the twentieth, not in the sixteenth, century. We strive to improve our standards of safety and purity, but we are still far from certainty in these vital areas.

One of the characteristics distinguishing man from the animal is his eagerness to use any agent proclaimed by anyone to ease his dis-ease. The agents are many. Anything from incantations to modern synthetic chemicals. Many rivulets formed as a result of this desire have become the torrents that are sooner or later poured, injected, swallowed, inhaled, annointed into the interior of almost every living person. For an increasing number this process begins at birth and lasts throughout a lifetime.

In modern times this broad stream of medication has become divided into four legitimate channels:

1. Over-the-counter drugs, which are supposed to be harmless in a proper dosage.

2. Drugs available only on prescription by a licensed physician and dispensable only at a licensed pharmacy or licensed chemist.

3. Food Additives, a growing and troublesome list of chemicals and drugs that may be added to food or fed to animals. Many of these are ultimately consumed by humans in varying amounts.

4. Fertilizers, pesticides and insecticides, many of which, through a circuitous cycle, starting with vegetation, animal consumption and digestion, ultimately enter the chemical processes of man.

From the beginning it became obvious that physicians by themselves could not control this increasing flood of drugs. It became apparent that government control in one form or another would have to be introduced. In Henry VIII's time, when most medications were sold by apothecary shops, control rested with physicians. This control was both inadequate and unfair to apothecaries. An attempt to reduce the myriad of quacks led to an act in 1525 that prohibited pharmacists from accepting a prescription written by a practitioner who was not duly qualified and registered. In addition the act specified that prescriptions were to be kept on file by the pharmacist so they could be examined by members of the College of Physicians to determine whether they were 'Medecynall or hurtful to the sickness'.

This might well be the first official attempt in the English-speaking world to regulate prescription drugs by government decree. But the triumph was short-lived; there were other interests that exerted political muscle. In 1542 the 'Quack's Charter' was passed. In its preamble it attacks members of the medical profession as 'Minding only their own Lucres, they have sued, troubled and vexed diverse honest men and women who without taking anything for their pains and skills have ministered the poor people for neighbourhood, for God's sake, and for charity.' God (by what process or instrumentality we are not told) had endowed these persons with knowledge of certain herbs, roots and waters, and with their use for customable diseases such as – 'sore breasts, pin and web in the eye, oncomes of hands, burns, scalding, sore mouths, stones, stranguery, saucefleme, and morphew and such like diseases'.* The charter provided that every subject of the king who had knowledge and experience of herbs, roots, and waters, by speculation or practice in any part of the king's dominions, might treat any 'outward sore, oncome, wound, apostemation, outward swelling or disease, by means of any herbs, ointments, baths, poultices, or plasters'.†

This charter suppressed effective control of medication by the medical profession for some three hundred years, when Food and Drug Acts and Poison Control Legislation were developed. Current experience with drugs and their adverse effects, even with the operation of Food and Drug Acts, indicates the heyday that

* Clark, Sir George, *A History of the Royal College of Physicians of London*, Clarendon Press, 1964.
† ibid.

charlatans enjoyed, and the risks incurred by the ill from all
varieties of healers, both licensed and unlicensed. Samuel Johnson, in his classic dictionary first published in 1755, devoted
considerable space to descriptive passages of various medications
in use in his time. Under the entry for 'Mummy' Johnson
borrows the following from a popular medical book of the time,
Hill's *Materia Medica*:

MUMMY – we have two different substances preserved for
medicinal use under the name of Mummy: one is dried flesh of human
bodies embalmed with myrrh and spice: the other is the liquor running
from such mummies when newly prepared or when affected by great
heat or by damps: this is sometimes of a liquid, sometimes of a solid
form, as it is preserved in vials well stopped or suffered to dry and
harden in the air: the first kind is brought to us in large pieces, of a
lax and friable texture, light and spongy, of a blackish, brown colour,
and often black and clammy on the surface; it is of a strong but not
agreeable smell. The second sort in its liquid state, is a thick, opake
and viscous fluid, of a blackish colour and strong, but not disagreeable
smell; in its indurated state, it is a dry solid substance, of a fine shin-
ing black colour, and close-texture, easily broken and of a good smell:
this sort is extremely dear and the first sort so cheap that as all kind of
mummy is brought from Egypt, we are not to imagine it to be the an-
cient Egyptian mummy. What our druggists are supplied with is the
flesh of executed criminals, or of any other bodies the Jews can get,
who fill them with the common bitumen, so plentiful in that part of
the world, and adding aloes and some other cheap ingredients send
them to be baked in an oven, till the juices are exhaled, and the em-
balming matter has penetrated so thoroughly that the flesh will keep.
Mummy has been esteemed resolvent and balsamick; and besides it,
the skull, and even the moss growing on the skulls of human skeletons
have been celebrated for anti-epileptick virtues; the fat also of the
human bodies has been recommended in rheumatisms, and every other
part or humour have been in repute for the cure of some diseases; at
present we are wise enough to know that the virtues ascribed to the
human body are all either imaginary, or such as may be found in other
animal substances; the mummy and the skull alone of all these hor-
rid medicines retain their place, in the shops.

It is important to note that all attempts at control have given
the qualified physician the power to prescribe or not to prescribe
the myriads of medications. Thus the physician has come to

stand as the guardian for his patients, protecting them from the thousands of offered and advertised remedies that range from the harmless to the dangerous, produced by those who seek wealth. Seeking wealth is not the only motivation for the manufacture, promotion and sale of drugs; but it is a motive as old as the hills and still dominant.

2 Research Varieties

The word research is one of today's glamour words. To every-thing – especially through the mass-media – it endows a charisma that may be converted to money. The mere mention of research in promoting autos, dogfood, drugs, soap, and so on gives the enterprise nobility. It conjures up the picture of silent, con-scientious scientists, covered by spotless white coats and sur-rounded by gleaming tubing, by liquids bubbling, by gadgets, meters, dials, blue and green waves running across oscilloscopic screens, and behind it all, a giant computer with small, white, flashing lights. It boggles the mind, but it wins in creating custo-mers for the product no matter what. Our society demands re-search. It gets it and pays through the nose, impartially, for the good, the bad and the indifferent.

A greater volume of effort is put into researching for new drugs than into any other research area. Accurate figures representing the financial input by the industry are impossible to obtain. The association of drug manufacturers in the United States advertises a figure close to one billion dollars for the year 1973. One firm alone, a giant of the industry, Hoffman La Roche of Switzerland, spent close to one third of that total on research. But figures can be misleading. This is mainly because there is no accurate defini-tion of what is really meant by the key word 'research'. It is fur-ther complicated by the fact that the amount of financial input into industrial research does not constitute a means of assessing its quality.

These figures do not give any indication of where these monies are spent. Nor indeed do they indicate whether these are gross (world) amounts or only the amounts spent in individual coun-tries such as: the United States, the United Kingdom, Canada, and others. One assumes that these vast sums represent world-wide research; but if one makes the alternative assumption that these represent expenditures entirely within individual countries, for example either the United States or the United Kingdom, that too would satisfy industrial aims.

One of the problems faced by the industry is the argument, within nationalistically inclined professional circles, that some countries, although sharing the burden of the costs of industrial research by the price structure of drugs, have little or nothing to gain from research laboratories situated abroad which employ foreign scientists.

For example: it is a sore point within some circles of the Canadian scientific and economic community that although the prices for pharmaceutical drugs in Canada rank among the highest in the world, there are very few industrial pharmaceutical research facilities within Canada. The bald argument is that the Canadian public is taxed by the industry for the costs of research, but sees little or no economic benefit from this taxation if the monies are spent in other countries.

The industry prefers not to enter into this area of discussion. Neither in its advertising nor in its hard-to-come-by financial statements can one determine where and in what amounts any individual country benefits economically from pharmaceutical industrial research.

In the industrial world the word 'research' is used in three separate ways.

To the accountant, the word, since it spells magic for government tax returns, means any expense that can be categorized as a research expense likely to be accepted as a deductible item against taxation. This opens a vast amount of peripheral activity – as distinct from hard-core research in a laboratory. It may mean the costs of holding numerous conferences with travel expenses, not only for the research workers, but for surveys of research activities being done in competitive centres. It includes the establishment of large reserves of capital to finance future research activities of the company. It may include the supply of very large amounts of expensive samples of the projected drug, during an early stage of its development, for tests on animals and for early trials on humans. For example, although thalidomide was never licensed for sale in the United States, Richardson-Merrel, Inc. had the franchise for the drug on the North American continent and supplied, without cost, 2,528,412 tablets of the drug under the name Kevadon to 1,267 doctors. All these steps are necessary for trial purposes. Despite this necessity, such steps often seem to invite free-loading and expense account largesse difficult to control and impossible to relate to a strict definition of scientific research.

To the sales departments of the industry research may mean market testing of a new product to determine its acceptability. It can mean saturation advertising in a circumscribed geographical zone, with special forays by company representatives into the area and special conferences to introduce the product and to test its acceptance by the profession, to which key clinicians and practitioners are invited at company expense.

To the scientific division of the firm research means what we usually mean by the word – the trial of certain chemicals or biological products in perhaps hundreds, if not thousands, of combinations and formulations to develop a specific drug that may be an improvement over existing treatment.

All these categories of research are essential to a firm before it can successfully market a product. But each category relates in a different way in the combination of the three categories. There may be a huge overload of costs in sales research, along with sparse efforts in clinical trial and equally meagre efforts in the scientific laboratory. There may be minor activity in the laboratory in order to create a 'me too' or a combination drug that is a simple chemical manipulation of a successful existing drug or a combination of two hitherto successful drugs into one entity. These may offer no clinical advantage to the patient but are capable of providing a 'new' patentable product. But vast amounts of money may be spent on this so-called research for marketing in order literally to overwhelm the medical profession into accepting this new drug as something vastly superior to the existing one.

Furthermore, even in the area of true research the definition is complicated by the different climates or styles of research. The distinguished biologist, S. E. Luria, divides this field of legitimate research into the 'Gee Whizz' and the 'So What' styles.

In drug research the 'So What' attitude leads to an end product. The inference in the question is 'So what does your idea lead to?' So what if you have discovered a new way of growing virus in a test-tube – will it now permit us to manufacture an improved vaccine for influenza? If you are unable to answer this question in the affirmative it is not likely that your research will be financed in an industrial setting.

The 'Gee Whizz' style is the one demonstrated by the kind of research scientist who says, 'Gee Whizz, I've got a question for which there is no answer and I want to work on it.' Here the object of an end product does not arise. There is only an itch to uncover a fragment of scientific truth. And out of this fragment of truth there may arise only another unanswered question – not a pill, not a treatment, just another question.

One cannot fault industry for being less than ardent towards the Gee Whizz research. There is no likelihood of immediate profit in 'Gee Whizz'.

In the allocations for research the 'Gee Whizz' types fight a rearguard action for existence – especially if the researcher is new and young in the field and is urged on only by a question. Up against a hard-nosed committee that has the duty to allocate research funds, the basic research of the 'Gee Whizz' variety does not endear. Sooner or later someone in authority will ask, 'Hey, where is the great breakthrough?' or, pointing to the pile of reports, asks, 'So what?' And yet, without the kind of question that may lead to further knowledge, science cannot survive. As examples, let us consider different kinds of research – each one oversimplified in order to emphasize the differences.

'Gee Whizz' and 'So What'

A research scientist, teaching in a university, is working quietly in the back room of one of the older buildings. Without industrial or government grants of money he is exploring an area that intrigues him and which may throw some light on a dark and minute area of protein chemistry, specifically on a fraction of the structure of the protein molecule. His equipment is little more than 'two safety pins and a piece of string', and some glassware that he has blown himself. He steals what time he can from his regular teaching commitment in his professorial appointment. He is operating with a minimal stipend from a special fund administered by his university department, intended to encourage this kind of personal initiative in research. He would experience difficulty in finding financial support through any of the other regular research funding agencies, because this kind of 'Gee Whizz' research is low-keyed, and a one-man type of operation. He works without the help of a technician and has no secretarial assistance with the exception of the regular departmental typist who takes pity on him and occasionally helps in making a typed script of his reports from his nearly indecipherable handwriting. He has been at this labour of love for four years and has not yet made any discovery worth reporting to any scientific journal.

Three years later, seven years from the start, he comes to certain tentative answers from his experiment, and from a close reading of related scientific literature. He writes a short 300-word report which he submits for criticism to the head and colleagues of his own department. Each member of this departmental research committee receives a copy of the report. There is an informal good-humoured meeting of sharp scientists, who tear into his reports and find two flaws in the set-up of his experiment, three mistakes in the mathematical calculations and one unsupported statement.

Two years later – nine years from the beginning – the above inconsistencies and miscalculations have been resolved and the research has now advanced to the stage where the report can be submitted for critical review by the research committee of the department of graduate studies of the university. It is approved for publication. Two years later – eleven years altogether – the report achieves print under the heading of Letters, in *Science* or *Nature*, both prestigious scientific journals. Acceptance for publication by these journals is considered an accolade in the scientific community.

Summary: in this piece of basic research, with a relatively

minute expenditure of research funds, a small but significant step was made towards an understanding of the protein molecule. A large expenditure of money on exactly the same research might have yielded an equally important answer, but in a shorter period of time. Or it may have yielded nothing at all. The nature of this research and its successful termination may well have been more directly related to qualities of mind and to the integrity, knowledge and persistence of a single research scientist rather than to any economic input, no matter how large or small.

Conclusion: The quality of research is not necessarily related to the amount of money expended. The quantity is.

Institutional Research

A research task force has been working on the problem of protein chemistry in a large, well-endowed research institute that has earned a solid, world-wide reputation for its scientific research. The task force includes a director (a Nobel laureate) and twelve research scientists, all of whom have doctorates in scientific areas, and all of whom devote full time to research. Many have international reputations based upon their previous scientific reporting. In addition there are twenty-two graduate students, working towards their doctorates, considered to be the cream of the crop, because they were accepted for graduate studies by the famous centre. There are in addition thirty-seven technical assistants each with a bachelor of science degree. The hardware is sophisticated and expensive: one piece of equipment alone was installed at a cost of one-half million dollars. Since its establishment this task force has produced never less than eighteen scientific papers each year, and in one year the figure reached twenty-nine. A scientific report under the imprint of this centre is accepted without delay for publication by any of the appropriate scientific journals. The editorial department of the centre, which finally approves the scientific papers before their submission to the journals, has three full-time writers, with doctorates in English, all with previous senior journalistic appointments. A secretary does nothing else all day but send reprints of previously published papers, written by members of this centre, in reply to the dozens of requests that arrive daily. The operating budget of this centre has never been less than two million dollars a year, has been rising progressively and has reached three-and-a-half-million dollars.

Summary: Flowing out of the research work of this centre, a stream of scientific papers has dominated the field of protein chemistry. Its quality cannot, of course, be related to financial return because it is not a business enterprise. Is there any other way of judging quality in this instance? Not really. The task force has qualified workers and all the other ingredients needed for research efforts on a large scale. But the question about quality is a variable that must be left unanswered.

Conclusion: While the methods of research can be judged by rigorous scientific standards, the results of that research, regardless of the prestige of the source, irrespective of the size of the endowment, cannot be judged in comparative terms. Much of it is stored away in publications and may later act as a stimulus to another research mind that may then occasion further research at some future date. Much of it, like Gray's desert flower, is destined to bloom unseen. Perhaps a very small portion of this vast effort fits somewhere into a scientific jigsaw that may end with a real substantial discovery or that may lead to a future Pasteur, Ehrlich, Florey, or Salk. But these occasions are very few. The rest remains in journals, piling higher and higher.

Each one of these reports represents painstaking, often extensive, research effort. The task of storing and then subsequently retrieving this ever-growing volume of research reports is in itself a subject of research, in which sophisticated librarians are involved, assisted by computer technology.

The volume increases year after year. There can never be a stop to man's inquiring. But in the scientific area the question must be asked: Are we reaching a point of diminishing returns with our burgeoning research efforts? How much research is becoming repetitious?

Because the retrieval of the reports of previous research in any scientific area has become so time-consuming and complicated, it may well be simpler and less laborious simply to proceed with a series of experiments to make the observation again, rather than expend an unpredictable amount of time discovering the reports of previous research on the same question.

The first limit to the amount of scientific research is the input of money assigned for this purpose. Such decisions are made from the consideration of certain priorities: how much on cancer, how much on heart disease, how much on nutrition with its related problems of environment pollution and need. The limits on the quality of research, as distinct from the amount of research, is an even more subtle and elusive judgement. The quality of research depends partly on money, partly on the scientific 'climate' of the area or of the country and partly upon policy decisions affecting the specific area of research, for example: cancer, cardiac disease, ageing and so on. But vastly more important than all of these is the quality and the integrity of the individuals involved in the research. It is this essential factor that is impossible to assess accurately in any concrete terms.

For these reasons the quality of research can never be related accurately to quantity of research nor to the amounts of money devoted to discovery of new drugs.

Drug Industry Research

To an ever increasing degree research leading to the discovery of new drugs introduced for medical use has become dominated by the larger drug manufacturing firms. This is a variety of research that in important respects differs from the research pursued in universities or research institutes. The goals differ.

In the university or institutes, generally speaking, research has as its goal the discovery of knowledge, known in the scientific community as 'basic research'. On the other hand in the industrial world it is 'mission-orientated' research that dominates. There the aim is to discover something of practical value, such as some advance in the treatment of a specific disease or the alleviation of a particular symptom. There the challenge is great – a cure for cancer or heart disease or something that has immediate usefulness. The risks, too, are great, both to the enterprise investing the money on this kind of research and to the individuals who are administered the new untried medication. But the proven rate of financial success has made both risks worth taking.

As a result a constant flow of new drugs appears on the market. These are distributed to the consumer in one of two ways: either directly, by over-the-counter sales, perhaps by simple request of the patient or upon the advice of the pharmacist – in the case of non-prescription drugs – or indirectly by being prescribed by the physician and then dispensed by a qualified pharmacist.

In either case a vast and increasing volume of drugs, frequently changing by reason of the nature of industrial drug research and marketing, is being consumed by individuals who do not possess the knowledge to enable them to discriminate. It is this absence of any real marketing choice by the consumer that makes the drug market unique and interesting – and profitable.

There is no doubt that great benefits have resulted from our new drug discoveries, particularly in the past fifty years. Evidence for this is readily available, and only the blindly prejudiced anti-drug person or the zealot supporting some form of drugless therapy would deny these gains. It would be a sad mistake to create regulatory controls so thoughtlessly or to apply them so rigorously that new drug research would become stifled. But this observation ought not to blind one to the very serious and often unnecessary risks involved in the commercially profitable exploitation of new drugs.

The Final Test

There are certain risks in the use of every new drug, particularly in the adverse effects as yet undiscovered because of the time lag in feed-back information. No matter how rigorous the laboratory procedures or the biochemical or physiological experimentation for each drug, no matter to how many guinea pigs, rabbits, rats, hamsters or baboons the new drug is administered, no matter how assured or predictable or beneficial the effects of such trials on laboratory animals are, there must still come the moment of trial on humans.

Trials on humans are risky and costly. They are subject to moral and ethical as well as medical surveillance. Merely to use the phrase 'human experimentation' conjures up memories of Auschwitz and Belsen and similar abominations. One of the darkest and most hateful chapters of so-called 'medical research' is the record of experiments conducted in Nazi concentration camps. As an example: the testicles and ovaries of adolescent boys and girls were subjected in an experimental way to increasing doses of X-ray radiations. They were then surgically removed for dissection and inspection under the microscope. The purpose was to determine the optimal dose of radiation in order to effect total and permanent sterility. Under cover of the currently acceptable moral and legal code then existing in Germany, it was desirable to rid the country of Jews and other ethnic groups forever, by making it impossible for them to procreate. To some in the Nazi hierarchy this appeared to be a more humane method of extermination, though slower, than what was practised in the concentration camps. Therefore in a moral climate that accepted *Judenfrei* as a legitimate goal, sterilization became a humane method to be preferred over incineration. There were other researches such as carbolic acid injections into the circulation, considered by some to be economically superior to the gas chamber. Hopefully these kinds of human experiments will not recur, assuming that there is not another mass descent into insanity.

But another kind of human medical experimentation must continue, or progress in drug treatment will cease. This is the kind of experimentation that must inevitably take place when the first, the very first, course of treatment with a new drug is carried out on a human, or the first surgical operation promising an improvement over the previous one is attempted.

Scientists, doctors, philosophers and legislators have agonized deeply over the moral issues thus raised. Working codes of ethics have been established, basically aimed to grant to the person experimented upon the free choice of acceptance or refusal. But frequently the patient is too ill, unable to comprehend the risk, too subject to the persuasive influence of people whom he trusts. The safeguard in all such cases is the moral and ethical equipment of the doctor who determines whether the trial ought to be carried out and upon whom. As honestly as he can he must balance certain non-quantifiable values: the degree of risk of the experimental drug against the serious risk of the natural course of the particular disease.

By way of illustration two opposing and relatively simple situations may be considered. A remedy is projected that is new and promising but known from animal experiments to have a moderately serious depression of bone-marrow activity, resulting in a significant proportion of deaths. The remedy is advanced for trial use for the common cold. To use the drug for this purpose would be wrong, even though the common cold can be a scourge to the individual and, by creating absenteeism from industrial productivity, an economic factor of important dimensions.

In another situation a new drug with similar hazards to bone-marrow formation in experimental animals nevertheless results in a significant reduction of cancerous growths. Here, of course, the moral considerations differ. The natural course of many kinds of cancer, left untreated, is radically different from the natural course of the common cold. In this instance, it is justifiable to accept the risk of experimentation. There is a vast difference between the use of an experimental drug intended to prolong life in an otherwise lethal disease and the trial of endless varieties of cold remedies or mood elevators, all having substantial risks to the trial subjects.

But more effort is devoted in the industry towards research in the area of fast sellers, for the potentially unlimited market of coughs, colds, pain relief, depressions, tensions, than to grim cancer. Prospects of financial success are immeasurably greater in the less grim group. Probably the most profitable drug of all time is the anxiety-relieving Valium. Human experimentation, when it was required for the development of Valium or other members of that family of drugs, was much less likely to have unpleasant consequences than when human experimentation is required for the trial of a drug for cancer. One can hardly fault a firm for adopting the less dangerous and more profitable group in its research. And so it is: 'Let's get on with that new sleeping pill, or that new thing to ease the burps.' That's where the research action lies and the money too.

Thus thalidomide. Forgetting for the moment that there were still unknown risks in 1959, it was indeed a very useful drug for tension and general nervousness and it was vigorously promoted as such. When sales on this basis soared, its market potential was given a further spurt when it was also advanced in Germany (where it could be obtained without a doctor's prescription) as being useful for insomnia, colds, coughs, flu, neuralgia, migraine and other headaches and asthma. Furthermore, sales received an even further substantial boost, when thalidomide became combined with other known drugs such as aspirin, phenacetin and quinine. The final touch was when thalidomide was advocated as the ideally safe drug for the nausea that occurs in the early months of pregnancy.

The windfall accruing to the company holding the patent for the drug thalidomide was astronomical. Can anyone compare this with the laborious non-profitable pursuit of the treatment of cancer?

Can one really blame a commercial company for seizing the one and ignoring the other? The question raises important, serious and fundamental problems, respecting not only the character of pharmaceutical industry research, but its funding and sponsorship.

The Volume

Certain distortions must arise when the primary motivation is profit maximization and where a sophisticated, shrewd marketeer determines company policy. At any point in time there are, of course, infinitely more people who suffer from the common cold than from cancer. There is literally no comparison between the prospective, potential markets. One can be counted in the millions, the other in the hundreds. Furthermore, the fundamental characters of the respective markets differ. The natural course of a common cold even without treatment is towards complete cure; the natural course of cancer without treatment is towards premature and sometimes painful death. A drug for the common cold, with an expected cure rate of only 10 per cent, has the glorious possibility of becoming credited with the cure of the remaining 90 per cent (which would have in any case become better). With the use of a drug for cancer a 10 per cent cure rate is a 10 per cent cure rate and no more. It is not just by accident or chance that a disproportionate part of industrial research and development in the pharmaceutical field has been directed towards treating ailments that are transient, fleeting and sometimes even trivial. In 1966 the United States Task Force on Prescription Drugs reported as follows:

The Task Force is convinced that the directions and quality of some industry research programs deserve careful consideration.

We have noted the serious and increasing concern expressed by practicing physicians, medical educators, pharmacologists and economists — and even some industry leaders — at the number of molecular modifications of older drugs introduced each year. Some of these modifications undoubtedly represent significant advances but most appear to be so-called 'me-too' drugs — substances which are not significantly different from other drugs, nor significantly better, and represent little or no improvement to therapy, but which are sufficiently manipulated in chemical structure to win a patent.

We have noted the comparable concern expressed at the number of new fixed combinations of old drugs introduced each year. Although these combinations may offer some convenience to elderly patients in particular, clinicians and pharmacologists have cautioned that they also involve obvious hazards and combine drugs in a 'locked in' proportion which may or may not fill the needs of individual patients. The number of duplicative and combination drug products introduced in recent years have been decreasing, but they still represent the great majority of all so-called new drugs.

It is evident that these duplicative products, along with combination products, are used widely by some physicians, perhaps on the basis of the industry's exceedingly effective marketing and promotion activities. But it is also evident that the need for this over-abundance of drug products has not been convincing to some medical experts.

In many of the Nation's leading hospitals, when expert physicians have served on pharmacy and therapeutics committees to select the drugs needed for both in-patient and out-patient therapy, they have generally found many, if not most, of these duplicative drugs and combinations to be unnecessary. These products have been found generally unnecessary by physicians providing medical care to the Armed Forces. They have been found generally unnecessary by leading clinical pharmacologists.

If these items were offered at prices substantially lower than the products they duplicate, they would provide at least an economic advantage, but in most instances they are introduced at the same or even higher prices.

The development of such duplicative drugs or combination products cannot be considered an inexpensive fringe benefit. Each requires laboratory research, clinical trials, and the accumulation of sufficient data to demonstrate to the Food and Drug Adminstration that the new product – although it may not represent any significant therapeutic advance – is at least safe and efficacious.

Since important new chemical entities represent only a fraction – perhaps 10 to 20 per cent – of all new products introduced each year, and the remainder consists merely of minor modifications or combination products, then much of the industry's research and development activities would appear to provide only minor contributions to medical progress.

The task force finds that to the extent the industry directs a share of its research program to duplicative, noncontributory products, there is a waste of clinical facilities needed to test the products, a further confusing proliferation of drug products which are promoted to physicians and a further burden on the patient or taxpayer who, in the long run, must pay the costs.

In the volume of its research endeavour the drug industry is unique. It spends a greater proportion of its revenue on research than any other industry. While other firms may be labour intensive or capital intensive the major drug firms are research intensive and the most important, the most expensive, the most respected part of their operation is in the research field.

The development of the modern pharmaceutical industry ended the importance of the frequently used 'snake-oil' types of medications. The new era of drug therapy started with research into the action of fine chemicals and biological products, vaccines, sera, etcetera. The early names in the drug industry are some of the greatest in the history of medicine.

Harry Wellcome came from the United States to England to found, with a fellow American, the firm of Burroughs Wellcome

& Company. He was a genuine and prophetic altruist. Recognizing the value of vaccines and sera, then just being reported in the research journals, he founded in 1894 the Wellcome Physiological Research Laboratories. Out of the revenues of his production company he attracted a unique team of scientists for basic research in the Research Institute, in areas that would not necessarily produce profits to his firm.

On his death he willed all of the profits of Burroughs Wellcome to the Research Foundation. In 1906 Henry Dale, one of the greatest physiologists of all time, became the director of the Wellcome Research Foundation and remained there until 1914, when he became Director of the Medical Research Council of the United Kingdom. During Dale's term in the Wellcome Laboratories he began his researches on histamines and acetylcholine, research that he carried forward and that earned him the Nobel Prize in 1936.

Koch and Von Behring – names connected with the discovery of the tuberculosis germ and with the treatment of syphilis and of diphtheria – were associated with the pharmaceutical firm of Hoechst in Germany. In 1935 Domagk, while with the Bayer Company, discovered the immensely important use of the dye Prontosil, the earliest of the sulphonamides, as the first true antibacterial chemical. He opened the important field of chemical antibiotic treatment of infection. The stars were almost to a man associated with the beginning of the drug industry.

The drug industry continues to spend more and more on research. But it has become a different kind of research from that of the Dales, the Ehrlichs, the Von Behrings and the Domagks. The costs of pharmaceutical industry research are so astronomic that they can be related to the public expenditure of vast amounts of money by governments and to the questions that such expenditures raise. When monies in the dimension of hundreds of millions are spent by any individual group, it invites inquiries – whose money? for whom? and for what purpose?

Whose money? Well, it is pretty obvious that it is the firm's money, honestly earned and legitimately applied to implement decisions from within the firm and subject to the firm's scrutiny. As for outside inquiries regarding the decisions on the subjects of research, the firm's attitude (as any firm's attitude) is – 'it's none of your business'.

Where does the money come from? The modern drug industry began with research. At first most of the research upon which the industry depended was done in research institutions or in universities. The amazing recent growth of the industry resulted from a shift in the geographic site, as well as the sponsorship, of the research directly to the drug firms themselves. Corporations developed sophisticated research teams for the kind of direct research useful for company goals. The value to the company of any specific kind of research can easily be assessed in money terms. It is research that either pays off or does not. The kind of research that does not pay off can be suppressed and the kind that does pay off will be sponsored. This conforms to an underlying imperative of all firms, and drug firms are not exceptional in this respect.

As this research becomes more and more profitable so more and more money can be spent on it. It is a perfectly safe and sure investment for a firm, once it has developed research teams that have conformed to industrial imperatives in their research goals. When the rules are observed, more and more millions can be poured into research – some of it useful to the public, all of it useful to the industry. But there is no doubt that the public pays for all of it.

Contrary to common belief the search for new drugs is not necessarily an integral part of drug manufacture. It is quite possible to separate the research function from the manufacturing process. One can conceive of an entirely separate research area that makes available its findings to manufacturing firms to process and distribute in a free enterprise economy. This would not differ greatly from other industrial manufacturing. There is much to be said for separating the research function from the profit-motivated manufacturing and distribution function in the drug industry. It could remove profit orientation from research and replace it with a genuine desire to advance the treatment of disease, whether it pays off or not. It could remove the stigma of over-concentration of research into the profitable areas of mood-altering drugs and encourage instead, research into areas where treatment lags. There are many such diseases even aside from cancer: diseases like multiple sclerosis and other as yet untreated nerve and muscle diseases, to mention only a few.

The allocation of large amounts of money to industrially orientated research invites critical scrutiny. The price of any drug on the market includes a healthy component for research as a charge to the buyer. These research monies are subject only to the control of industrial management. This assessment for research can be compared to a tax. If research is an essential part of the manufacturing process, then the assessment is indeed a compulsory tax, imposed by a private firm on the purchaser of the drug.

There are other ways whereby this research tax could be collected by representative government and distributed for new drug research to existing research establishments in recognized universities, or research institutes, established for this specific purpose. Under the existing system, when this tax is collected by industry, there is a compensatory reduction of government funds for university or institutional research. The result is a continuing drain of research brains into the industrial area and away from research institutes and universities. Given the choice many, perhaps most, well-trained and well-motivated research scientists would prefer the university environment to the industrial firm. But with the growing trend to more industrially sponsored research and less money for university research the drain goes on.

Promotion and Research

It is impossible to discover how much that is forthrightly promotional goes under the label of research. Is the sending out of tons of samples justified under a kind of research label, because doctors are encouraged to try these on their patients for the first time?

There is a large and very expensive area of drug promotion that masquerades as a kind of continuing education for the sake of the practising doctor. It has almost completely displaced genuine post-graduate medical education conducted by universities or medical schools. Most members of the practising profession have come to depend upon this kind of industrially inspired continuing medical education. It uses the language of sophisticated research, it impresses and in a superficial way it satisfies the average practitioner beguiling him into believing that he is keeping abreast of the most recent developments in genuine research.

Thus, in one glossy brochure, advertising to the doctor a drug for urinary (kidney and bladder) infection * the following three statements are quoted out of context from three separate medical-journal articles. Each statement, it should be noted, says nothing positively about the promoted product; but each one knocks a competing group of drugs.

About penicillin: 'This may kill the bacteria by removing their outer defences but it can – and often does – result in the survival of L-forms.'

About sulphonamides, trimethoprim, and nitrofurantoin: 'Each of these antibacterials blocks only one specific step in the process. Although a sulphonamide with trimethoprim exerts a sequential double blockade between para-amino-benzoic acid, dihydrofolic acid and tetra-hydrofolic acid, as with a single agent, this blockade may be by-passed without detriment to the bacteria.'

About tetracycline and chloramphenicol: 'Though the ribosomes are the assembly plant of the cells, their function is controlled by DNA. Unless this control is knocked out, the cell functions are never completely destroyed.'

To the average doctor this language of scientific research is impressive enough to sound like real educational material. Even when he does not understand it, it may make the sale.

But what is even worse, this fruit of the advertising copywriter serves to satisfy the need the practising doctor feels for continuing education; it has largely diverted attention away from post-graduate education sponsored and directed by established educational institutions. The enormous cost of this kind of thing, where the teachers are company representatives or detail men or

* A multicoloured brochure including a post-paid sample offer extolling Negram, published by Winthrop Laboratories, 1974.

even advertisements in medical journals and direct mail brochures, is, of course, born by the buyer or by the taxpayer, in the
form of additional impositions on the price of the drug. It would
be handled best by regular educational channels, teaching hospitals, medical schools and universities. A doctor's education is not
really benefited by the industrial marketer or by industrial goals.

Surely, in a matter as important as education of doctors in
practice, industrial slanting should draw strong objection from
professional associations. Could it be that professional associations themselves have become an integral part of the industrial
promotional machine?

In 1970 a symposium on the marketing of pharmaceutical
products was attended by representatives of most of the large
firms. The following is a quotation of one of the statements made
by a spokesman for the industry:

All of us recognize the end purpose of our efforts in the area of
physician typology. It is to identify those segments of the physician
population which contain our best customer prospects ... By far the
most important criterion is estimated or observed prescribing volume
. . . overall prescribing productivity ... When we compared prescribers and non-prescribers . . . it emerged that non-prescribers
thought the patient's condition less severe than the prescriber. It is
not inconceivable that one could devise a strategy which questioned
the doctors' interpretation in these cases.

The above language is contorted and not easy for the average
person to comprehend. However, what it does convey is the industry's desire to bend the doctor who prescribes less frequently
into prescribing more and more. A distinction is made between
the doctor who assumes, based upon history and examination,
that the illness is not serious and may, therefore, not require any
medication, and the doctor who is inclined to medicate for
practically everyone that he sees.

It is obviously the aim of industry to convert every doctor into
the automatic prescribing category. The *Lancet*, in an editorial
dated 23 March 1974, had this to say:

The pressure on doctors, in effect if not in intention, was to treat
rather than to observe and educate, and to treat symptoms rather than

disturbed physiology. The association of virtually every doctor – patient contact with a prescription had deep historical roots that could be torn out only with great difficulty; but the effect of pharmaceutical marketing was to drive them deeper and make them flourish at the expense of cautious and rational care.*

Whose money, for whom, and to what purpose? It is public money used for industrially directed research and promotion, with the sole aim of selling more and more pills to increasing numbers of consumers, irrespective of real need. The system operates very successfully. To attempt to dismantle it for the public good is a daunting challenge. To put the question boldly: Is it better for society to supply the vast sums the drug industry needs to continue its search for more pills, or would it have been better to have devoted an equivalent amount of money to basic research into the biology of the cell?

Pills and Basic Research

We are all made aware of the very large expenditures on research by the drug industry by widespread propaganda and publicity. Henry Simmons, Director of the United States Food and Drug Administration, stated that the American pharmaceutical industry in 1972 spent six hundred and eighty million dollars on research (50 per cent more than it spent five years previously). Well-placed advertisements in leading journals stated that in 1973 the Drug Manufacturing Association of the United States spent close to nine hundred million dollars on research in that year alone. Under existing marketing drives this figure is likely to escalate year by year. To many of the decision-making areas of government this seems magnificent. To the legislator these amounts are impressive. In these important spheres of influence money for research, whether it comes from private industry or out of government revenues, is properly recognized as originating from the consumer's pocket. But in these circles it is often a matter of indifference whether the money is allocated to finance research by industry or given to universities and research insti-

* Lancet, 1974, i, 490.

tutes. As long as it is ear-marked for 'research' the end seems to be right and the means without significance.

If basic research is ignored, the pool of basic scientific discovery, the source for any other kind of research, drys. There must be a pool of basic information before the 'break-through' in the 'wonder drug' field is possible. The important areas of chemotherapy and antibiotics required vast amounts of research labour in discovering basic information about the properties of chemicals and the biological identification and characteristics of moulds, etc. The Salk Vaccine could never have been discovered without basic research in nutrient media – the soup in which micro-organisms can be grown so that they can be identified. Penicillin and the entire field of antibiotics arose out of a chance observation of the effect of a contaminated culture that deterred the growth of a common micro-organism.

The continuing danger to the essential requirement of basic research is the confusion of the decision maker held in spell by the word 'research' and the uninformed assumption that all research is basic. Dazzled and delighted by industrial propaganda about the vast amounts spent in the private sector of research, he is disinclined to give high priority or government funding for basic research. This has been the sad story of government support for basic and medical research in nearly all the countries where industrial propaganda about research is widely spread and generally accepted.

3 People

Quick Quick Relief

The rapid rate of technological progress inevitably leads to the belief that for every situation relief is readily available. For every need there must be fulfilment. To many, this is what is meant by rising standards of living.

But with rising expectations come the tensions and the struggles for fulfilment. We have been led to believe that for every disease there is a remedy. We expect and demand freedom from any form of anxiety or psychological tension. In short, we demand to feel good throughout the wakeful part of the day, to sleep soundly at night, and to awaken refreshed, full of zeal and the eagerness to cope. We demand total freedom from any pain or discomfort, even for the shortest period. The 'common cold' is no longer tolerable. We expect the anxieties that come with the tests of life, the examination, the interview, the decision, the marriage, the bereavement, and so on, to be made free from discomfort and dis-ease.

We have been taught and conditioned to believe that all of these rough situations can be made smooth by the appropriate medications. Only the deprived, the ignorant or the miserably poor need suffer; and in a sense they suffer because they are indeed ignorant, deprived or poor. For the rest of us, who are 'with it' and intelligent, there is always quick relief from any of these troublesome occasions, no matter how transient or trivial.

It may be, as claimed by some behaviourists, that this demand for 'quick quick relief' begins in the cradle with the use of soother and goes on through appropriate use of alcohol and cigarettes as tension relievers. Were these agents all that were required to relieve our tensions, the pharmaceutical industry would be much smaller and involved only with research and development of drugs that may influence real organic and metabolic disease. The market for so-called psychotropic drugs would not have developed except for use in established mental illness.

But the market opportunity in fulfilling the demand for quick quick relief from anxiety and transient discomfort was too inviting to be ignored for ever by the marketeer in the pharmaceutical industry. From the conditioning provided by the soother, cigarettes and booze, it was only a short step to the vast potential market of products that could be claimed to make you 'feel good' under any kind of circumstances, even if you no longer resorted to soothers and did not rely on cigarettes or booze.

By no means is this to say that psychotropic drugs do not have a distinct area of proper medical use. Thousands of helpless individuals, who might otherwise require institutional care, are today leading socially useful, if not exactly happy, lives by the administration of active psychotropic drugs in proper dosages by their psychiatrists and general practitioners. Indeed, it is the success of these drugs in producing dramatic and obvious change from helplessness to hope in so many, that has demonstrated to the marketer the massive potential market that exists. If one of these drugs made such a difference, obvious for all to see, in Aunty Elie, who for years was afraid to move out of her room and who now attends family gatherings, why should it not be as good for me, when I feel like hiding from my examination, my interview, my husband or my wife, from my children or from my employer? We all confront thousands of occasions when we say to ourselves: 'If only I could escape for a while!'

Well, escape is here and readily available. The marketer has taken full advantage of this market. The advertising sections of medical journals are full of glossy advertisements for these mood-affecting drugs. If you are tense and distraught, there are soothing drugs. If you are simply depressed and inert, there are mood-elevating drugs. Samples and literature to practising physicians clog the mails and fill the shelves.

There are perfectly respectable approaches to acquiring these agents. The best of these is from the doctor, who will presumably tailor a particular pill to your particular needs. And it need not only be the anxious moment for which you are seeking his help. It may be vague discomfort, or a headache, or a cold or merely a check-up. If, as in most cases, the doctor finds no evidence of organic or metabolic disease, his immediate concern is to end the interview and to get on with his next patient. The quickest and most acceptable way to end the interview is to write a prescription. In far too many instances the prescription is for one of these psychotropic drugs or for an antibiotic. This course of action is more the result of the massive promotion for these groups of drugs than any positive conviction the doctor has, regarding their value in every single case for which he prescribes them. But the interview must be terminated in a respectable and mutually acceptable manner.

You take the little pill and indeed feel better – as you might have with a soother or cigarette or booze – with the advantage that there is less social or medical stigma to taking a pill prescribed by a respectable doctor. The market booms as a result of the repeat prescriptions.

Not only have we become conditioned to taking pills for ordinary life situations, but we lose – or perhaps never acquire – any real experience with personal and individual handling of life's anxious or critical moments. We lose or never develop the capacity to cope with the examination, the interview, the forthcoming dinner party, the visit of the mother-in-law, the common cold. Not only do we lack the experience or the confidence to handle these occasions, but we never learn how to become 'patients' in any acceptable meaning of the term. We are inclined actively to seek medication for everything we confront, and what we seek we get from the doctor or from over the counter in a near-by drugstore or chemists. The drug market continues to soar.

The public is not simply a passive receiver of all the medications it swallows. While there is active collaboration between industry and the medical and pharmaceutical professions, there is manifestly a ready and eager acceptance by the public of whatever medication is offered. Scepticism may occasionally erupt on the part of the receivers of all these 'goodies', but on the whole it is people who actively seek treatment and who receive the medications who consume more and more.

There are profound historical and anthropological roots for the conviction that for every malady or for every symptom there is an external cure or a relief by some form of treatment. We have become conditioned to accept that there is indeed a state of perfect health. Our notion of what is 'normal' centres around this concept of blooming, perfect health. Furthermore, we accept without question that perfect health is a steady state, that it exists or ought to exist for every day for every hour of our lives until somehow we come to a natural end. In pursuing this ideal we are quick to accept any nostrum, any treatment that promises quickly to remove the occasional discomfort or the periodic transient illness. There is no way that the average person can separate the simple symptom such as a cough or a pain in the back or in the belly – the trivial and the transient – from the serious or the lethal. There is no certain way for the individual accurately to answer this question, except by consulting the experts in this field – the physicians.

To complicate the doubts there are two factors, both important. The first is the variable state of individual anxiety. The second is related: the duration of the symptoms. All the evidence provided by the universal sharp increase in the cost of health points to growing mass anxiety regarding health. We are consulting doctors more and more frequently and as a result receiving more medication than ever before. In spite of improvements in nutrition, in sanitation, in spite of the virtual disappearance of some of the serious diseases that used to plague us, tuberculosis and poliomyelitis, and others, we are not 'healthier' if costs and amounts of pills consumed are any indicators. On the contrary the rapid increase in the need for the psychoactive drugs (tranquillizers, sedatives, etcetera) or the tons of antibiotics prescribed could lead one to assume a deterioration in health.

Part of rising expectation about health is that we have been sold a chimera, a piece of cloud nine. On top of our basic assumption that there is indeed a state of perfect health, we believe we can achieve it only by taking the appropriate treatment – the sooner the better. The emphasis in this notion is on some form of drug treatment.

Up With Homeostasis

There is, in medical jargon, the concept of 'homeostasis' – an important word about which many are unaware. It is not exactly translatable into everyday English. Neither Roget's *Thesaurus* nor the *Oxford English Dictionary* include this word. Even medical dictionaries give it short shrift. Stedman's medical dictionary says 'the processes through which bodily equilibrium is maintained'. It means, reduced to simple terms, the truly astonishing capacity of the body to heal itself with no external intervention or medication whatsoever.

Some scientists call this complicated biochemical and physiological process – automatically set into motion for self-healing – 'the wisdom of the body'. Be it a single celled amoeba or a complex multi-organ structure such as the human body, no living organism could have possibly developed, let alone survived, without this capacity. Whether it is an injury, an infection, a growth, the process of homeostasis is there to intervene, arrest the danger and restore the organism to its normally healthy equilibrium. This, without our having to lift a finger, let alone swallow a single pill.

By far the overwhelming majority of ailments that occur in the course of our lives are quietly, efficiently and almost predictably eliminated by this watch-dog process within all of us. We are frequently conscious of the operations of this process by a feeling of soreness or pain, or fever or thirst, or any of the myriad of common symptoms that indicate to us that we are undergoing dis-ease. But in most cases we can be confident that our homeostatic process will effect cure without requiring outside help.

In some cases the processes of homeostasis are overwhelmed or retarded and external help, in the way of some form of medication or treatment, is clearly and definitely needed. There are some critical jobs that homeostasis is unable to do. It can arrest the small haemorrhage but we need surgical help to stop the big one. It can overcome the minor infection; the major one requires the appropriate antibiotic. Homeostasis will erase the minor tensions from the frequent and common stresses of life. A major depression will require special treatment by suitable medication. Homeostasis will not limit the growth of a malignant tumour.

In these areas intervention is required. The entire panoply of the health system is designed to operate in just those areas and in those diseases where homeostasis fails. Not every pin prick requires treatment and no medical system could withstand claims to treatment for every single incident transiently affecting the equilibrium of the individual.

Socially useful health systems are designed to do two things. Firstly they are designed to distinguish those conditions that the body itself can handle without any external intervention – so diagnosis should determine and sort out those ailments that demand medical help from those that do not. Secondly, health systems should search out the causes of and provide suitable treatment for the conditions that have escaped the self-healing capacity of the human body.

At any given moment in any community there are two reservoirs of illness. The first one is the largest and is made up of a constantly changing population. This is the reservoir of illness that is adequately handled and cured by homeostasis. There is a large stream of individuals constantly entering and an equally large number constantly leaving this reservoir. From the point of view of the economics and logistics of medical care (the supply of doctors, nurses, hospital beds, and so on) the greatest boon to society would be some magic device – some simple test – as yet not discovered, that would select quickly and surely the individuals that belong in this category and provide them with kind words of reassurance, plus perhaps faith in the value of a cup of hot tea with lemon, but nothing more. Above all no drugs. But to arrive at a diagnosis when a disease is at its earliest stage can be a daunting challenge for a doctor. All doctors must rely, in most ailments, on being able to appraise, in retrospect, the progression of a portion of the natural course of the symptoms of a particular disease. Immediately at the beginning of a pain it is extraordinarily difficult to diagnose what is wrong – whether the disease belongs to the first or the second category. The earlier the visit, the greater the difficulty of diagnosis. Fortunately, not all diseases demand early treatment. Except for the few that by their severity require immediate care, most symptoms can safely be left to efficient homeostatic processes for treatment without requiring external intervention by surgery or by medication. This is the reservoir of illness that is bedevilled, aggravated and to an increasing degree converted to the seriously ill by reason of useless medication or unnecessary surgical treatment. The history of medicine is full of crazy nostrums and absurd operations that were at one time or another inflicted upon individuals exhibiting these harmless self-limiting illnesses. How many hundreds of thousands of tonsils, of appendixes, of uteri, of ovaries, have been surgically removed from citizens who temporarily found themselves in this group at a time when these procedures were advocated and performed within the then accepted practice? But removed they were, as any doctor who practised a mere twenty-five years ago can testify. Fortunately the surgical mayhem inflicted upon individuals in this group has almost completely ceased, because of improved standards of control in hospitals where these procedures must be performed. But the same cannot be said for the medicines and pills that are swallowed by this group of individuals with illnesses certain to be cured simply by homeostasis.

For the energetic entrepreneur this group forms an ideal market. Their numbers are very large and becoming larger. Their ailments will disappear and credit for the disappearance of these ailments will go not to homeostasis, about which the consumer knows nothing, but to the pill that comes recommended by the most respected of persons, either the pharmacist or the doctor, and manufactured by an ethical, reputable firm. As the record has abundantly shown, any enterprise that can penetrate this market quickly arrives at the élite stage in the industrial empire – from the twin points of view of profits and prestige.

But to penetrate this market is not easy and requires capital resources that are enormous. One must be prepared to invest very large amounts of money in research. One directs a large part of the research into the ailments that occupy this reservoir of self-

limiting illness. Examine the announcements of new drugs resulting from the research of the larger manufacturing firms and
appreciate the dominant emphasis placed upon research in the
mood changing drugs – drugs to provide sleep for the restless and
drugs to elevate the spirits of the depressed. Since most of the
patients who complain this way have mood swings that are very
close to normal – the mood swings that all of us experience – the
great majority of these medications are unnecessary. Improvement will as assuredly follow without drugs as with them. To a
significant number in this group of patients, drugs only impose
the added hazard of adverse drug effects.

To this huge group of the non-ill (who, periodically and for
variable durations, merely feel rotten), the industry has directed
special attention: subtle phrasing in the advertising to the doctor
is used to convert him to prescribing the promoted drug for the
non-illnesses. Even if your patient feels only a teeny-weeny bit
anxious and you don't want to sedate him or her, Presto! 'Have
we got the exact drug!' The advertisement is headed in prominent letters, 'Effective control of symptoms without undue sedation'.* It is a statement that varies, depending on an analysis of
its significance, from the meaningless to the misleading. If one
is treating a patient for real crippling anxiety – and occasionally
one does – then the proper medication is one that does indeed
sedate and sometimes unduly. To state that anxiety can be
treated by a sedative pill 'without undue sedation' is either a
hoax or toying with words. And yet this statement was repeated
over and over again in the promotional literature for a particular drug directed towards doctors who can be induced to believe
that they can now, with this new wonder drug, treat anxiety by a
sedative pill that does not carry the risk of 'undue sedation'. This
opens a vast market for the thousands of mildly anxious patients
whom the doctor might hesitate – and rightly hesitate – to treat
with sedative pills. Now at last – Eureka! – a pill that does not
cause 'undue sedation'.

Another rich market for pills is the mildly anxious patient who
visits the doctor more than once. The model in the promoters'
mind is constructed like this: A doctor may see a mildly anxious

* Adv. *New England Journal of Medicine*, 16 May 1974.

patient once and does not prescribe. But when she (the advertiser nearly always uses the female sex – they're much more attractive in the illustrations) appears more than once then: Zapp – she gets the pill. It can be left to the psychologist to determine how much male chauvinism is involved in the head-line of an attractive multicoloured brochure that illustrates the same lady in full length six times and proclaims:

You've talked . . .
   You've listened . . .
      But there she is again*

and on the overleaf:

'Again' . . . and 'and again'.*

The whole thrust of this kind of psychological gamesmanship is to get rid of the patient who keeps coming again and again. If the patient becomes dependent on the drug for the rest of her life, well, that's the name of the game. If she develops adverse reactions, well, there are other drugs to treat these.

The second reservoir of illness is much smaller in number of patients and relatively constant in size. It includes all those within the community who have either life-threatening ills or ailments that are disabling. This group is not too difficult to define and the average doctor has little problem with diagnosis here, after the illness has progressed to some extent – although treatment is another matter. Research into this group of illnesses is difficult, expensive and agonizingly slow.

It is understandable that the public, unaware of homeostasis, unaware of the intricacies of basic research, is bedazzled by the great advances proclaimed by the industry for the commoner, self-limiting illnesses. Why tolerate a cold, or flu, or a cough, or a headache, or just feeling rotten if only for a day, when relief is so obviously and abundantly available merely for the asking. For the doctor to counteract this massive propaganda is difficult although not impossible. Above all, it is time consuming. Yet the growing problem of unnecessary, undesirable and even at times

* Mailed brochure distributed by Smith Kline & French (Canada) Ltd, 1974.

dangerous therapy cannot be fairly blamed on the public. We are what we are – tense and worried targets of the promotional blasts of the drug industry. The amount of health propaganda to which we are subject, both overt and covert, is truly enormous.

Apart from advertisements there is an endless flow of articles, many inspired by public-relations writers for the industry, that paint glowing word pictures about the goodies in pills, if only we would avail ourselves. The message of the heart transplants conveyed to the public was not that of a procedure introduced for humans too soon and without adequate research. It was a message of 'Gee-whizz, if they can do that they can surely cure my cold or my tension or my headache.'

Serenity is a word too old-fashioned and irrelevant in our modern society. It has too little place in our notions about health. And yet an injection of serenity into our concept of what is involved in health would create attitudes more important than the discovery of a new tranquillizer, sedative, or sleeping pill, and much less adverse reaction.

Pill-Popping to a Drugged Society

The rapidly spiralling use of drugs in modern society is truly astonishing. Never before have so many taken to swallowing so much. Proof of this is all around us – the importance and strength of drug companies in the industrial empire and in particular among the giant multinational corporations. The stars of the stock exchange are aglitter with drug companies. Astute observers, looking either for rapid appreciation in market value or for long range growth of investment, have relied upon and rarely been disappointed with the selection of drug-company investment stock.

Like other constellations of industrial stars the large multinationals in the drug industry have had an important influence in the growth of satellite stars. Among the gainers are: the advertising industry, pulp and paper, radio and television – all performers whose contractors depend upon advertising – fine chemical companies (a large part of whose productivity is devoted to the ingredients of the active drugs or the accompanying solvents or diluting agents); the glass, plastics and container industries; and the transportation industry. These and others would be seriously adversely affected if the drug industry were to be restrained.

The pace of life, tension, the acquisitive society, the rat race, subconscious or conscious fears associated with greater knowledge of disease and its possible catastrophic consequences have all been implicated. Not even a ninety year old is allowed to die from natural causes. Death, according to our mechanistic concept of life, comes only from some disease affecting an organ or an organ system. Well-meaning groups that sincerely want to help the victims of heart disease, cancer, arthritis, cystic fibrosis, diabetes, muscular dystrophy, multiple sclerosis, mental disease, and many others, all have their fund-raising offices with full-time staff whose primary function is to conduct public drives to collect funds. Through all the media we are reminded of the occurrence of disease. There is no doubt that these drives have a beneficial effect on the funding of research foundations. The other side of the coin is that the fear of disease is kept in constant focus by the concentration of attention upon disease.

Fear is still the greatest spur to action. Fear of illness is a powerful emotive force and its influence on the individual is probably permanent. The same fear that impels one to fight cancer with a 'cheque or a check-up' remains as a permanently conscious or subconscious zone of anxiety. Fear drives many people to repeated check-ups annually, monthly, even weekly, for the slightest or most trivial reasons. We have become conditioned to be ready and eager to swallow whatever may be prescribed to allay the fear.

Drugs breed drugs. Take the pill – the one that prevents conception. The fear of pregnancy is of course the reason why many millions are taking the pill, and there are perfectly valid reasons based upon economic, sociological and health grounds to avoid pregnancy. But even with the knowledge that the pill is nearly one hundred per cent effective, the anxiety is not forever ended with the swallowing. One may shift the direction of the anxiety. There are known hazards to taking the pill. These are widely, perhaps too frequently, proclaimed in the press, radio, television, and discussed with horrifying examples at coffee klatches and morning telephone visits. The very occasional – indeed on the basis of relative frequency, the excessively rare – instance of a serious undesirable effect from taking the pill (thrombo-embolism – the occurrence of clots in veins and their dislodgement in the general circulation) is discussed and agonized over until it becomes its own primary focus of anxiety. Who can blame a woman taking the pill, subject to these influences, from wondering if that stabbing pain in the chest, fleeting but there, represents the lodgement of one of these clots with possible dire, if not catastrophic, effects. Or is it just one of the varieties of minor, transient, generally unexplainable and equally unimportant aches and pains to which we are all subject? Some sturdy, perhaps uninformed, or unimaginative, or stoical characters will ignore it. Many will not. They will respond to their anxiety by a visit to the pharmacist or the physician. In either case they will emerge with a bottle or box of something. More swallows, more profits. The sophisticated marketeer is not unaware of the importance of anxiety for creating market opportunities.

The Elderly – A Special Target

Sleeping and ageing have proven to be bonanzas to the marketer. Wherever it is permissible, especially designed broadcasts are beamed to particular audience groups, the elderly, the housewife, even children. These programmes are directed to special advertising goals: vitamins for the elderly, sedatives for the housewife, and especially concocted breakfast food for the children.

Older people, especially in America, are frequently ashamed of getting old. Anything that may be done to stave off that dread period when one is old is bound to sell. All that is necessary is to broadcast the message to that particular age group. The advertised product speaks of eternal everlasting postponement of old age.

Another advertised nuisance of getting older is so-called 'sleeplessness'. A large segment of the population will not accept the reality that sleep is variable, just like the frequency and timing of bowel movements. The myth drilled into us ever since we were young, that we must have eight hours of sleep each day and every day, is as deeply ingrained as the myth that regularity of bowels is a prime and noble achievement. And so – notwithstanding the plain fact that older people require and get less sleep – a sleep market is created with programming directed to the elderly. Salvation is offered for the sleepless: 'quiet, restful, splendid sleep'. All that is required is a simple pill.

When the astute advertising executive surveys this area of hopeful belief, he sees an imperative for exploitation. That is his job. He relies on real emotional forces to work for him; he can exploit fear and he can exploit gullibility, in addition to simple ignorance.

Jane is a pleasant seventy-six-year-old widow, childless, and left in a reasonably secure financial condition by her deceased husband, who suffered a sudden, fatal heart attack. She represents a very large group of retired persons, financially independent though not wealthy. She lives in a comfortable home she shared with her husband. There is no outstanding debt on the house and she has managed to keep it in good repair.

How Jane happens to live out the rest of her life depends almost entirely on what happens to her health. Crude as it may sound, if Jane were to die suddenly she would be spared many problems. A desperate problem that can reduce the Janes to near beggary is the problem of paying for medication in a country where there is either no public assistance for medication or where public assistance is inadequate.

In illness the Janes are entirely at the mercy of three factors. Over none of these has she any influence. The three are: a disease; a drug company; a doctor who makes the choice of drugs for her. Jane's health and happiness depend on these factors. Sadly the cards are stacked against her. She is a helpless thing, tossed about by great impersonal powers. There is a remote possibility that compassion may exert its effect. But the drug company cannot be compassionate; no commercial firm can be and continue to exist. The firm can only establish its profits or fail.

There is no middle course. On the other hand Jane's doctor is a compassionate person and is a member of a humane profession. The historical roots of the profession grew out of the stuff of compassion. The doctor ought to know Jane's precarious position in an industrially directed consumer society. He knows about the adverse effects of drugs in general, he knows the cost of drugs, whether paid for by Jane herself or covered by an insurance scheme or by a national-health scheme.

But when he writes a prescription for Jane his action is determined by many other factors that dominate and submerge compassion. He can prescribe only what he knows, and he knows what has just been told to him by that apparently knowledgeable company representative about the great new breakthrough in the treatment of Jane's condition. He was prepared for this information, perhaps even eager to receive the company representative, because several weeks ago he had read a report of a trial of this very drug in a mail announcement directed to him from the firm. Impressive scientific jargon in the article was hard to follow, but the concluding paragraph confidently stated that 'this drug was a clear advance over previous treatment'. The doctor did not notice that there were no 'double blind' * comparisons of this drug with a dummy drug nor with the existing drug he had relied upon previously. Nor did he analyse the closely tabulated figures in the body of the article that did not support the optimistic conclusion regarding this drug. Nor did he see other reports of other trials of this drug appearing in other journals that were less than enthusiastic. He did not receive the other journals. It would have required periodic visits to a medical library, from which he was separated by a considerable distance. Nor was he aware of more recent studies reporting rare but serious adverse effects. These included skin rashes that proved particularly difficult to treat and disturbances of liver function and bone-marrow depression, resulting in some cases in a fatal anaemia. Nor did he read the package literature, issued by the manufacturers of the drug, that listed accurately, but in tiny print, all of these possible hazards.

If Jane lives in a country where the cost of drugs is borne by the public purse, there is another kind of hazard. Because there

* See p. 122.

are only minimal financial restraints to prescribing, Jane can acquire prescription drugs more frequently and in greater volume and variety than in a country where the drugs would be paid out of her own purse. The British Health Service theoretically exercises continuing surveillance over the prescribing habits of individual doctors. The records show a progressive increase in the per-capita consumption of prescription drugs. There is little if any evidence that the surveillance has had any effect on reducing either the prescribing or the consumption of drugs. The record of prescribing by the individual doctor is compared by the authorities with the average for all the doctors in a designated area. But the average has been continually rising. The individual doctor has to be grossly extravagant in his prescribing to exceed the rising average. The result is more and more drugs that find their way into the insides of patients and a steadily growing reliance by the Janes upon drugs.

There are many circumstances that tend to exonerate the doctor. He was not at fault in those instances where there was failure to convey important information to him, relating to the safety of the drug. As a result of the many occasions when he did receive the message that the drug promoters wanted him to receive, he had become an essential, but unwitting, cog in a sophisticated system, skilfully engineered to sell that particular drug. Without the doctor's compliance, this system would fail, and so extra special care and much money is devoted to achieve professional compliance, the goal of industry being to direct the hand of the one who writes the prescription.

The promotional system leading to the climactic prescription depends upon a single, ever-present hazard in a doctor's day – the time factor. Truthfully and literally, he cannot find time to devote to his patients and also do the proper and essential searching out of new information that would disclose to him all the facets about this particular new drug, bad as well as good. To the extra demands upon his time he answers the most pressing: the crying child, the injured victim of an accident, the more seriously ill, the acute demands of the depressed, the distressed, the miserable, the frightened. All these claims and many more must be served before he can find time to search out all the details about a new drug. He would not be a doctor if he had any other order of priority. The patient comes first.

The promotional system of the drug company provides instant information in impressive variety and frequency: the glossy advertisements, cleverly and intentionally designed to catch the eye even before the scientific article catches the eye; the ubiquitous polite, pleasant representative, who waits patiently in the waiting room on the chance of a five-minute informal chat about what's new. What doctor has the heart to send him away? The representative has waited patiently for perhaps as long as an hour and will leave on the desk a bundle of goodies – free samples, that can be given to the poorer patient, pencils, key rings, memo pads, and so on. Then there are the displays at the medical convention, with information pleasantly and conveniently packaged, and the entertainment rooms in the hotel where one can meet old friends and have one or two agreeable drinks as guests of the drug company.

All these factors will help to determine what the doctor will write on the prescription he gives to Jane. And write a prescription he surely will. Not that he must or that he even should: but he will. Jane is frequently in his office, not because she is ill, but because she is lonely and depressed and frightened, or because she has just been advised to see her doctor because there is a cancer-detection campaign – and the television, radio, press, plus the women's magazines have insisted that Jane see her doctor to discover whether she had an early cancer about which she herself cannot possibly be aware – or because Jane has become accustomed to seeing her doctor once a year or once a month or once a week. To break the pattern becomes unthinkable. Or Jane has been told by the doctor to see him again in three months or three weeks or three days. Or Jane is worried about a nagging, recurring pain in her abdomen, or her back, or her chest. Or Jane has suddenly lost a dear friend from a heart attack, and the post-mortem telephone conference between herself and other friends concludes that the dear and suddenly departed friend of eighty-six had not been 'looking after herself' and Jane decided that from now on she will 'take care'.

These and dozens of other reasons have filled the doctor's waiting-room with many Janes and Henrys, all waiting patiently to consult the doctor – far more than he can properly attend to. The only way they can all be seen is by rationing time, and time rationing goes on in every doctor's office – except perhaps for the few months at the beginning of his professional life. Rationing time means that Jane has just so much of the doctor's time and no more. Then he reaches for a prescription pad and starts to write.

Technology and Perfection

Increasing demand for drugs, indeed increasing demand for all kinds of medical care, is related to the inevitable effect of increasing technology.

All about us there is evidence of technological change that aims to provide perfectly functioning equipment. Through the years our autos operate more and more quietly and, hopefully, are almost trouble free. When they are not, someone has boobed. When we buy the automobile we are assured by industrial propaganda that the design is perfect. Therefore, if there is malfunction somewhere along the assembly line, a mistake has been made and this mistake is discernable and capable of correction. Moon shots provide an example to each of us that it is indeed possible to invent, design and manufacture intricately functioning equipment that works predictably and has built-in devices that automatically detect and correct aberrations in function. Even the human body is about to be repaired by replacement of malfunctioning parts, kidneys, blood vessels, even heart. We, all of us, doctors as well as the public, accept a mechanistic view of life. It fits with the engineering concepts that surround us in our environment.

If rising expectations give us a vision of total technological control over our environment, why should this control not operate over the human body? It would require only the application of a biological formula like the technological one that has worked so efficiently for the machine.

And so arises the urge to apply mechanical principles to health.

It means that we define health in the mechanical terms of the orderly working of organs. We can easily slip into this definition, especially when every other definition becomes vague and deals with spiritual and philosophical concepts. And the mechanistic view is in line with the evident objective world of things around us.

Why then should there not be a pill for everything – for every discomfort, every disease, every sniffle and cough, and for every health problem? If there is not now, at this moment, there must be one just around the corner. When a prestigious drug corporation calls news conferences to make an announcement of yet another important breakthrough, we have become conditioned to accept it, not with scepticism, but with joyous alacrity – not with sales resistance, but with eagerness. For every ailment there must be a cure and for every ailment, every symptom, we immediately head for the nearest drugstore or the nearest doctor. And so the sales of over-the-counter drugs boom, and the visits to the doctor become more frequent, and we are in perpetual need for more and more doctors, nurses, technicians, hospital beds and a thriving industry to provide more and more hospital supplies and pills.

It is a kind of perpetual motion machine that is revolving at a continuously increasing pace. All this is a kind of 'weltschmerz' a world sickness, easier to diagnose than to cure. The forces that propel this machine are not easily subject to change. Can we do anything to re-educate the public about health, so that the antibiotics or sedatives are not the inevitably expected conclusion of a visit to the doctor? Can we dismantle a machine made up of giant multinational corporations whose very existence depends on the growth of the machine, not its dismantling? Can we do anything about 'rising expectations of health', induced by more drugs that promise to set our human machines right?

There may be a glimmer of hope – now that payment for health in many countries with publicly financed health schemes is swallowing up larger and larger bites of gross national product. Studies are quietly going on regarding 'cost benefits'. Are we getting our money's worth, or are we just being beguiled into mistaking activity for improvement? Is there real, hard-nosed, scientific evidence of improvement in total health, definitely improved life expectancy and reduction of disease? Is the impressiveness of the intensive care unit, designed for the care of the acutely ill heart patient, really providing an extension of comfortable life – or are we merely confusing the more for the better?

4 What's Doing with Drugs?

VITAMIN E: A Drug in Search of a Disease

Given the prevailing eagerness of the mass of humans to consume anything offered on the pretext of making one 'feel better', given the general state of scientific knowledge about the action of drugs, it is not too difficult a task for the drug company to sell the public almost anything. Nor has it proven difficult for the marketers to convince many medical practitioners that anything developed by the ethical drug firm must be good.

Take as an example Vitamin E (Alpha-Tocopherol). It is enjoying an amazing popularity in both over-the-counter and prescription sales. The most authoritative statement on Vitamin E was written in 1970 by Sir Stanley Davidson and Reginald Passmore in the fourth edition of their standard text book *Human Nutrition and Dietetics* (Williams & Wilkins, Baltimore) as follows:

Vitamin E is one of those embarrassing vitamins that have been identified, isolated and synthesized by physiologists and biochemists and then handed to the medical profession with a suggestion that a use should be found for them – without any satisfactory evidence to show that human beings are ever deficient of it or even that it is a necessary nutrient for man.

This makes Vitamin E a sweetheart in the world of drug industry promotion: to first produce a product and then invent the disease for which it can be vigorously advanced.

Vitamin E is a very interesting biochemical, known to enter into the structure of the cell membrane in human biology. In no way has a deficiency of this vitamin ever been identified in the human. It occurs in large stores in human fatty tissue and even though special diets have excluded Vitamin E for months on end there is enough in the human storage depots to sustain adequate levels. For these reasons imagination and promotion could be allowed full sway without the restraints of factual knowledge. With no supporting scientific evidence whatever, Vitamin E has at one time or another been advocated and sold in ever increasing quantities for one or more of the following conditions or uses:

Ageing, acne vulgaris, after-shaving tenderness, allergies, amyotrophic lateral sclerosis, angina pectoris, atherosclerosis, cancer, chronic cystic fibrosis, chronic cystic mastitis, coronary heart disease, cosmetic skin conditions, diabetes mellitus, frigidity, habitual abortion, hemolytic anaemia, hypercholesterolaemia, infertility, lupus erythematosis, macrocytic anaemia, muscular dystrophy, myasthenia gravis, peptic ulcer, rheumatic fever, scleroderma, under-arm deodorant, venous thrombosis.

Furthermore Vitamin E has climbed onto the mega vitamin wagon. It has no known toxicity, no matter what quantities are consumed. Therefore the certainty of obsolescence encountered with other drugs (in order to create new sales for the succeeding new one) does not apply to Vitamin E. The same effect can be achieved by substantially raising the dosage of Vitamin E from the conservative levels to the much larger or mega-dosage. This elevation to senior-dose status also has the advantage of substantial increase in price without further investment in research. Thus the recommended dietary requirement by the Nutrition Board of the National Research Council (United States) was 5 units for infants, 10 to 15 for children and 20 to 30 for adults. It is not possible for an individual, assuming there is no serious and prolonged intestinal disease, to get less than those amounts in any ordinary diet. In spite of this, and absolutely without scientific evidence, it has been promoted as a preventive for heart ailments with dosages from three hundred to one thousand units daily. Many thousands are on these dosages either with or without the advice of their doctor. The industry happily supplies this demand. This widespread medication and wasteful overdose of Vitamin E gives many a false feeling of security and creates situations where proper medical care is postponed or denied.

Fortunately the stuff is harmless to the human body. But that is all that can be said for it. Its damaging effect is indirect: to syphon-off monies that could be put to better use. It perpetuates the age-old fallacy that health is available only by swallowing something – anything. See the quotation on 'Mummy', to discover if we have advanced in this respect.

Antibiotics to the Rescue

The typhoid bacillus has been with us for a long time as a murderous cousin to the hitherto harmless E.Coli. Typhoid fever has ravaged armies and decimated populations until basic sanitary measures – generally separating human sewage from drinking water and milk – have made the disease relatively rare in developed countries.

Occasional sporadic epidemics and individual cases still occur. These are almost invariably traceable to a carrier, plus a breakdown of sanitation. In rare cases an individual who has recovered from typhoid fever, perhaps in a mild unrecognized form, has become resistant to the germ that continues to live secretly within his or her body and may thus infect others. There the development of antibiotics – specifically chloramphenicol (Chloromycetin) – has come to the rescue. The death rate from established cases of typhoid fever has by this development become significantly reduced and epidemics, although alarming (because they really ought never to occur), are not nearly as lethal as they were.

The tricky way in which occasional individual infections may occur is illustrated by a single case that happened in a Canadian city several years ago.

A Jewish Orthodox widowed lady, who maintained a strictly kosher kitchen, accepted, at the request of her synagogue, a temporary house guest – an equally orthodox Cantor who had arrived to train the synagogue choir. In about ten days the Cantor became seriously ill and a diagnosis of typhoid fever was established in the hospital. He readily recovered with the administration of chloramphenicol. Because this was the only isolated case of typhoid fever in this city for many years, public health authorities were determined to discover the source. The carrier was quickly traced to the good lady who maintained a strictly kosher and clean kitchen.

Invariably typhoid fever is transmitted from a human source – either someone who has the active disease, or from a carrier who is not aware that live typhoid germs are present within his or her body, because the state of being a typhoid carrier can be consistent with normal good health. In this particular case this perfectly healthy, orthodox, Jewish lady, was proven to be the carrier of live typhoid germs. These were transmitted to her equally orthodox house guest in a totally innocent manner. Even following normal conscientious hand washing, some germs remained in the nail areas of the fingers and were passed on in the preparation of the food. (Remember that surgeons scrub their hands for seven minutes by the clock and wear sterile rubber gloves in order to be certain that no microbes will pass from their hands to the patient.)

There is general agreement that the greatest improvement in health and, in turn, the length of life, when measured from birth date, has been in that very large group of diseases called infections. As a result of this improvement, millions are alive today who would not have survived one hundred years ago. This, more than any other factor, has created the population explosion of modern times.

This improved outlook for survival – thirty years has been added to life expectancy when measured from birth during the last century – was created by three factors: improved sanitation, better nutrition and the discovery and wide distribution of drugs to counteract infectious diseases.

These three factors are inter-locked and it is not possible to attribute superiority of one over the others. Safe water and pure milk are essential – but so is resistance to infection from improved nutrition. But at least equally important have been antibiotics in curbing infections at the earliest stage. These reduced the large reservoirs of infection among neighbours that used to exist in pre-antibiotic days.

Whenever epidemic infections do occur, however, there is nearly always a breakdown in sanitation or nutrition. Antibiotics then are important to reduce the death-rate and stamp out the infection.

A serious spread of infection where such a breakdown occurred was an epidemic of typhoid fever in Aberdeen, Scotland, in 1964 affecting 515 individuals. All but eight of these cases occurred over the short period of just five weeks.

The failure in technology that was the primary cause of the epidemic was discovered by super-sleuthing by public-health officers. This, no doubt, brought the epidemic to an abrupt end. But the availability of the appropriate antibiotics accounted for the amazingly low death rate in this epidemic – three deaths out of 515 cases. Prior to antibiotic days conservative estimates placed the mortality at 10 per cent. In other words if antibiotics had not been available there would have been at least fifty-one deaths in the Aberdeen outbreak instead of three. Furthermore it is altogether likely that many more cases of typhoid fever would have developed were it not for antibiotics. In an epidemic antibiotics not only cure more victims but, because those afflicted carry the germs for a much shorter time, the reservoir or pool of infection is sharply reduced.

The epidemic in Aberdeen occurred because of a breakdown in South America of two technological details upon which the framework of sanitation rested. A modern factory processed meat and packaged it into six-pound tins of corn beef especially for export to the United Kingdom. The plant in South America was a model of sanitary engineering and techniques. No greater attention to antiseptic detail is observed in a modern hospital. In order to ensure absolute safety and sterility of the contents each tin was vacuum sealed by metallic seams and each tin was then sterilized by pasteurization. This recognized and respected method required that every sealed tin of corn beef be heated to just below boiling and then rapidly cooled.

This particular plant made economic sense by using as the cooling agent an adjacent cold natural stream. About half a million people lived up stream and raw sewage was dumped into it. It was considered, by the responsible authorities, that the metallic sealing of the vacuum-packed tin, plus adequate chlorination of the cooling water, were more than adequate to protect the contents.

But there entered into this scenario two unpredicted events that broke the chain of safety in South America and caused the 515 cases of typhoid fever in Aberdeen. Firstly, during the cooling stage – because of the increased stress on the metallic seals caused by the intensification of the vacuum within the tin – a tiny pin hole occurred in only one of the tins. The hole was too small to allow any of the content to escape – but large enough to permit a drop or two of the cooling water to be sucked into the tin. Secondly, no one knew that the chlorination plant – intended to sterilize the water containing the sewage of half a million people – had not been operating for fourteen months. Typhoid fever occurred periodically among the population along the stream.

The cycle of events creating the epidemic was completed in a modern supermarket in Aberdeen. There a mechanical slicer cut across the six-pound block of meat, depositing typhoid germs on the surface of the knife. The same knife was used to slice other cuts of cold meat. Between them the first portions of the sliced South American beef and the spread of contamination to other cuts, were responsible for 515 cases of typhoid fever and three deaths.

The lesson from these tales is that reduction of infectious diseases requires the coordination of social and technological factors affecting nutrition and sanitation in addition to the final guardian, the antibiotic drug – not just the drug alone, important as it is.

How Now Brown Cow with DES

Nowhere in the world are drugs more scientifically and accurately administered than in the animal world. The goal is single and direct. It is to make the animal more productive in economic terms. No one has to bother how the animal feels, nor does one even have to consult the animal on this important human point. The troublesome 'placebo' effect never gets in the way. If an animal's condition is improved by the use of any drug, it is clearly the drug that is the responsible agent. It is not any mysterious psychosomatic response between patient and doctor or patient and pill. If there is any effect, it must certainly be due to a predictable pharmacological action. In animals scientific controls of dosage can be accurately assessed, and the influence of other factors, such as food or other drug effects, are either minimal or easily subject to scientific calculation. In scientific terms the variables can be reduced to a minimum. No emotion, no liking or disliking of the doctor, no having a quiet 'snootfull of booze' consumed secretly, prior to the administration of the tested drug, no having been recently chewed up by an angry spouse, ticked off by a demanding boss, jilted by a lover — these and other hidden variables do not occur in the treatment of animals.

For these reasons interesting and potentially profitable effects may be quickly and accurately achieved on the controlled administration of drugs to animals. For example, soon after antibiotics were tested on animals, it was noted that not only did they recover from whatever disease for which the antibiotics were used, but the control animals — perfectly healthy beasts — who were given the same antibiotic gained weight appreciably and profitably. This started a surge of experiment in the use of antibiotics in the diet of animals solely for the purpose of weight gain. Feeding antibiotics to animals thus became a standard procedure in animal husbandry for the purpose of achieving increased revenue. For the producer it was a straight economic calculation — the cost of the antibiotic in the feed as compared to increase in income. If the figure is favourable, the antibiotic is used and both the manufacturer of the drug and the producer of the animal are made happy.

For the human consumer there are other considerations. Trace amounts of the antibiotic appear in the flesh of the animal. When the meat is eaten there is insufficient residual antibiotic remaining to produce any noticeable medicinal effect on the individual, but enough to possibly sensitize a potential patient to that particular antibiotic. Should the patient then have that antibiotic administered to him at some future date, one of two effects may occur: either an immediate allergic reaction such as skin rash, vomiting, diarrhoea or collapse may complicate the illness for which the antibiotic was administered; or, alternatively, a total failure of any beneficial effects from the administered drug, because the germ being attacked has developed resistance to the specific antibiotic used. In either case these minute trace doses of antibiotics appearing in the meat may prove disastrous to the individual who has a critical infection, demanding the use of that particular drug.

Industrial goals sometimes conquer human interests. Vast amounts of antibiotics have been sold for animal feed in many countries in spite of proven hazards to individuals. The sale of antibiotics may be carefully screened and controlled in drugstores and chemist's shops and pharmacies, where they are administered to humans. But they may be easily obtainable without a doctor's prescription in many feed stores, may be fed to the animal, and arrive at your dinner table with the meat.

A second effect harmful to humans, resulting from the feeding of antibiotics to animals in meat production, comes from changes occurring in the gut of the animal.

There is a very large family of micro-organisms called E.Coli that live normally, happily and indeed usefully in the human gut. A good deal of the breakdown of cellulose fibres in our diet is activated by these friendly germs and much of the Vitamin B essential to human nutrition is manufactured for us in this way, right inside our own gut. Over many centuries – since man became a flesh eater – we normally have, in that portion of our gut called the colon, the same breeds of E.Coli that exist in the gut of the animals we have become accustomed to eating.

Although it may seem repulsive to man, there is an inevitable transference of the gut content (during the killing of the animal and dressing of the carcass) directly onto the meat that we eat. Innumerable microscopic tests have shown the presence of E. Coli on the surface of perfectly edible meat. While most of these are destroyed in the preparation and cooking of the meat, enough raw or under-cooked meat is eaten to have provided over the centuries a second home for these beneficial germs inside the human colon.

With the administration of antibiotics to farm animals in their feed, the effect on these peaceful innocuous families of E. Coli, that we have lived with for centuries, has been injurious to humans. One or both of two things has happened to this gentle micro-organism. It has either been killed off by the antibiotic or it has developed cousins that are resistant to the antibiotic. In either case what now exists in the guts of many of us is no longer the mild innocuous brand of E. Coli, but vicious microscopic disease creators. These breeds are now prevalent in hospitals. The special circumstances that bring together a large number of the ill, at a time when their nutrition may be impaired, their resistance low and when they are recumbent, create an environment favourable to the spread of their micro-organisms. There is evidence that such organisms do arrive in the hospital via the diet kitchens and can be spread among the hospital population. These micro-organisms have become permanent residents on hospital bed-pans, mops, toilet bowls, sinks, etcetera.

In this manner multiplication of infection can occur from a single source. Fortunately not every person who comes into con-tact, in one way or another, with these micro-organisms develops disease. Most of us carry our own antibodies or resistance to specific germs or, luckily, less than the minimal number of germs enters our bodies. Less than minimal amounts do not form a colony and therefore do not survive. For these reasons, even though infecting agents always surround us, only comparatively few of us suffer disease. But the possibility of hospital infections originating from meat as a result of prior feeding of antibiotics to animals is disquieting.

Some of us who are getting small amounts of animal-feed antibiotics in our diets are becoming insensitive to the beneficial effects of antibiotics generally. Much has still to be discovered through basic research concerning immune reactions. This is a complex area that includes two elements. The host reaction – not only to the invading germ but also to the defending antibiotic – is a highly intricate subject demanding much research. In addition alteration in the germ itself as it reacts to the antibiotic is a fur-ther complicated, mysterious and largely unexplained region.

Until more is discovered in these intricate but promising fields of basic research, the human consumer remains at risk, while the feeding of antibiotics to animals is permitted for economic reasons.

A further intrusion into the privacy of the placid cow is the addition to its feed, again for weight gain, of the hormone

DES (diethyl stilboestrol). The most interesting factor about DES is the example of how long delayed may be the effect of agents, chemical, hormonal and physical, on the human. In the case of DES it is the second generation and only the female side that gets clobbered. This ought to raise genuine ire in the Women's Liberation Movement. In most countries the feeding of DES to agricultural animals has now either been stopped or is rigidly controlled. But the damage may already have been done and may not become evident for many years.

It has become known that cancer of the vagina may occur in the daughters of mothers who have received DES during the pregnancy. Significant is the long delay in harmful effect and its involvement of a total innocent in the transaction. The animal does not suffer, it gains weight and receives its inevitable reward, slaughter for increased profit to the producer and food for the consumer. The pregnant mother eating the DES-contaminated food does not suffer on this account and gives birth to an apparently healthy female. It is this offspring, when grown to adolescence, that is at risk of developing a hitherto excessively rare tumour: cancer of the vagina. This disquieting piece of evidence of the next generation being at risk lines itself alongside thalidomide, except that this one takes even longer. Thalidomide babies sadly, and too obviously, declare themselves at birth. DES takes more than ten years longer. We do not know yet whether there will be an upsurge of human vaginal cancer as a result of the amounts of DES already given to animals. But even the anxiety that this threat creates does not contribute to any improvement to public health.

Our society is more and more beset with trade-offs. The drug industry proudly proclaims boons to public health, and the agriculture industry, assisted by the drug industry, proclaims increasing productivity. On the other hand the public must trade off these advantages against growing concerns about future health, added to the current social costs of adverse drug effects.

There's Gold in Them Thar Pills

Growth has been spectacular in the drug industry in the past twenty-five years – and so have profits. The amount of monies involved in the sales of the products of drug manufacturing is impossible to calculate. This is due to the fact that the major firms are multinational, operating in countries where different laws apply regarding disclosures required from commercial firms. For instance Switzerland, where several of the larger firms operate, has protective legislation that shrouds financial affairs in mystery.

In addition to the difficulty of accurately estimating the money value of drug sales, there is the problem of the definition of 'drugs'. Drugs for human consumption, drugs for veterinary use, drugs sold over-the-counter on a doctor's prescription, drugs used as cosmetics, deodorants, herbicides, defoliants, drugs stockpiled for chemical warfare, certain chemicals used as food additives, some drugs freely sold in one country that are illicit in another: all these factors prevent the gathering of accurate figures regarding the total sale of drugs for human medical use.

The major drug-manufacturing firms are mostly within the élite known as multinational firms. The multinationals have financial strength that in many cases exceeds that of many governments. Their total sales have been estimated at five-hundred-billion dollars annually. The growth rate of multinationals is twice that of the growth rate of the gross national product of the entire world. The liquid assets of the multinationals has been estimated to be two hundred and fifty-eight billion* by the United States tariff commission and one hundred and thirty-eight billion by the First National City Bank of New York. These sums are greater than the financial reserves of many countries. Each of the ten largest multinationals earns annual revenues greater than the gross national products of two thirds of the countries of the world.

Furthermore, many of the multinationals are conglomerates in various markets, with products varying from chemicals closely

* One billion equals a thousand million.

related to drugs to chemicals for war-time use or crowd control, and even to services as remote as hotels, car hire, and others. To extract out of the financial statements of say International Telephones and Telegraph Company an accurate statement regarding sales and profits from pharmaceutical drugs would daunt even the nimble brain of a Harold Geneen.*

Nevertheless, the sales of drug companies have been reasonably estimated. There are several clues to this. One is the reporting by some of the larger firms to the shareholding public, with recorded prices of shares on the stock market. Over the longer term, share prices reflect the firms' profits either established or anticipated. For many years drug stocks have been favourites in the stock exchanges across the world.

The total turnover of drug sales in 1971 has been estimated conservatively as sixteen billion dollars, with the leader of the pack a Swiss firm, Hoffman La Roche,† doing a turnover in 1971 of one thousand two hundred and fifty million dollars. Number two in the field was the American conglomerate, American Home Products, doing a thriving sale in drugs of eight hundred and two million dollars. Even number twenty-two in the list, British Beecham, hit a respectable one hundred and forty-two million dollars.

This is not to fault the companies because of giant size. It does give, however, some idea of the financial power of the larger companies and the immense aggregate power of the industry to ward off any threat. Previously the only threats to profitability have come as competitive threats from each other. But, by the kind of interlocking arrangements, by licensing agreements between each other, by observing divisions of exclusive territory for marketing purposes, and similar kinds of manoeuvres consistent with a megalopoly, competition between the giants has been eliminated.

* Anthony Sampson, *The Sovereign State*, Hodder & Stoughton 1973, p. 16.

† It was reported in 1974 that Hoffman La Roche alone spends more than £100 million ($230 million) annually on research. It is estimated – but not confirmed by Hoffman La Roche – that this amount represents about 15 per cent of the total amount received by the Company in sales. This calculates to an annual turnover of approximately £700 million or $1·7 billion (approximately). (London *Observer*, 28 April 1974.)

Actions by various governments, for example the British Government against Hoffman La Roche* or the American court action regarding the manufacturers of tetracycline†, have been mere pin pricks, in spite of the substantial millions they have cost the companies, when compared to the total financial base and profits of these giants.

As for profits, one can surmise again – because accurate figures are impossible to obtain – but one need not weep! The United States Task Force on Prescription Drugs (1968) reported:

In a free enterprise system it is obvious that a company must make a profit. Unless it achieves this primary objective, it cannot stay in business. Ample evidence is available to demonstrate that the drug industry has been able to stay in business. It has maintained an annual profit based upon net worth which is substantially above that of the average major American industry. . .

Spokesmen for the drug industry have agreed that its profitability is above average. They say however that this rate is necessitated by the high degree of risk in the industry, and the need to attract the capital to finance their growth.

The Task Force has been unable to find sufficient evidence to support the concept that the drug industry is a particularly risky enterprise.

There is abundant evidence that the development of an individual drug may be associated with a high degree of risk, and that any such development is an economic as well as a scientific gamble. There is, however, no evidence that this type of risk characterizes a typical major drug company with a substantial line of drug products. When such a company undergoes a painful loss in this kind of gamble, the record would seem to show, it generally covers it by substantial profits in other drugs.

The record would also tend to show – at least during the last twenty years – that losses of this nature have driven few if any major pharmaceuticals manufacturers into serious financial straits.

In recent years, some major American manufacturers have diversified their operations by moving into other operations. In some instances this has been described as an attempt to minimize risk. At the same time however, it is apparent that other companies are diversifying their operations by moving into the drug field.

* See p. 81.
† See p. 77.

The chief economist of the Federal Trade Commission has testified, on the basis of advice given by investment analysts, that there is no reason to conclude that the drug industry is an uniquely risky industry. In fact, it appears that the large drug companies should have little difficulty in obtaining adequate capital for growth should they choose to go into the market for it. Actually, however, their earnings are large enough to preclude the frequent need for equity capital.

Hardly ever does the industry have to go to money markets for additional financing. Most pharmaceutical corporations generate sufficient cash flow and a high enough profitability to have easy access within their own reserves to adequate funds for any new ventures, any new lines of research, any vigorous promotions or marketing plan – no matter how costly – any excursion into any new market. If losses occur – occasionally they must – they can be easily recovered in the pricing structure of the succeeding drugs.

These giants are cosy and secure. Penetration into their select market requires such vast amounts of capital, so much in expensive and rare human resources, so much marketing and promotional expertise, that whatever is available in these rarefied areas has already been absorbed by the major firms. All that less wealthy firms in industry can do is either look on with envy or allow themselves to be brought into the conglomerate take-over game. Dr John M. Blair, the Chief of the Federal Trade Commission Division of Economic Reports (United States), presented the following figures (on a scale of one to a hundred) as a comparison of rates and returns after taxes in selected industries (1957):

Drugs	21·4
Industrial Chemicals	16·2
Office and Store Machines	15·5
Motor Vehicles	15·5
Glass	14·9
Electrical Machinery	14·2
Engines and Turbines	13·5
Abrasives, etc.	13·3
Soap	13·0
Petroleum Refining	12·8
Tobacco	12·6

Steel	12·4
Dairy Products	11·9
Bakery Products	11·4
Tires and Tubes	11·3
All Manufacturing	11·0

For many years the profits of the drug industry have been twice the average for all other American industries.

Figures and statistics are frequently confusing. Perhaps the dimension of the drug industry can be determined from the following example. Thalidomide in the United Kingdom was manufactured under licence by Distillers Corporation, a conglomerate that in addition to its major enterprise – the manufacture and sale of whisky and other liquors – entered into product related areas such as pharmaceutical drugs, one of which was thalidomide.

The published figures of 31 March 1972 showed Distillers to have a capital of four hundred and twenty-four million pounds. This amount includes a lump of 24·7 million pounds in solid cash. The accounts also show investments with a market value of 42 million pounds. In addition the accounts disclose unquoted holdings estimated by the directors to be worth 10·6 million pounds. These investments alone produce for the company an income of 2·5 million pounds. And this was only 3 per cent of Distillers' pretaxed profits. In addition, 247 million pounds worth of maturing stocks of liquors were owned by the corporation on that date.

It cannot, of course, be argued that all this represents the wealth of that segment of the conglomerate that manufactures thalidomide. What it does indicate, however, is the size of the giants who are in the business of making and selling drugs.

What chance then has a consumer who is ill or a group of consumers representing the ill? In considering size or wealth or power, how can any consumer or professional group be anything more than a Mickey Mouse along side these financial giants?

Of the three areas working in the field of public health – government, industry and the medical profession – the power of the large corporation greatly outranks the other two. Watergate, if it revealed nothing else, indicated the amounts of covered money transferred from industrial giants to the very highest level of the political arena. While Watergate was distinctly an aberration, there is little doubt that election campaigns are enormously expensive – not only in the United States. Supporting funds must be gathered from sources that have money in such amounts. It is naïve to assume there is no quid pro quo. The transference of such monies from industry to politicians creates obligations. It is not possible positively to track down the money given to a politician for his campaign and to relate this to any specific act by government in trying to compare the quid with the quo. Watergate contained a strong suggestion of a commitment by International Telephones and Telegraph Company to contribute four hundred thousand dollars to the 1972 Republican campaign at a time when an antitrust inquiry was in progress. Watergate also uncovered a substantial contribution by the Milk Producers' Association of the United States that was followed closely by a government-approved rise in the price of milk.

Enormous leverage upon politicians who make up goverments can be brought to bear for specific goals desired by the drug industry. This kind of leverage is available only to the industry – not to professional groups and certainly not to consumers. The uncomfortable conclusion may be drawn that by degrading the medical profession to the position of voluntary or passive sales agents – and by the financial power which it exerts upon politicians – the drug industry has made the public, particularly the ill, sadly exposed and without protection.

Tetracycline – The Public Backlash

Under the United States Consumer Protective Legislation there is a type of legal action known as Class Action. Within this area a legal firm may, at its own risk, institute an action seeking restitution and damages for an unstated group of consumers. To win such an action (and incidentally, more than compensate the costs to a legal firm) the lawyers must prove to the satisfaction of the court that consumers suffer financial or other losses in the purchase of a particular commodity. The amount of money claimed must be related to the total amount of over-pricing – whenever over-pricing is alleged. In turn, this amount relates to the total sales of that commodity within the area under the jurisdiction of that particular court. In summary then, one clue to the number of transactions and profits accruing from the sale of a particular commodity can be found in those Class-Action cases where the litigation has been resolved and the financial compensation for losses determined.

The action taken in the United States against the manufacturers of one antibiotic – tetracycline – can serve as an illustrative example. Tetracycline belongs to a group of drugs known as broad-spectrum antibiotics. These are usually obtainable by prescription for human use to counteract infections against a wide range of germs. For ordinary prescribing, where doctors cannot, without time-consuming tests, determine the specific germ causing the infection, the doctor is most likely to order one of the broad-spectrum antibiotics. Of these, tetracycline is the most popular because of its effectiveness and comparative freedom from adverse effects (nausea, diarrhoea, rashes, and so on). The demand for tetracycline as a prescription drug is very high. The price was set, not with the usual competitive market factors prevailing, but by whatever figure the accounting departments of the manufacturers set. It is a part of the advantage to the industry from the development of an oligopoly. A small number of firms, licensed to manufacture the drug and sell it under their own trade names, combine upon a uniform selling price – to remove the profit-eroding effect of price competition.

In the United States about one hundred and fifty civil actions were started by various groups against five companies – Pfizer, Cyanamid, Bristol, Squibb (a division of Olien Mathieson Chemical Corporation) and Upjohn. Out of these one hundred and fifty actions, sixty-six were consolidated and an offer of settlement for these sixty-six was finally approved by a United States district court on 18 September 1970 for an amount of one hundred million dollars (approximately forty-three million pounds). This staggering amount of money involved in the over-pricing of tetracycline cleared less than one half of these actions. With the fixed settlement of well over one hundred million dollars for less than one half of the action, it has been estimated conservatively that before all of the remaining actions are completed the total amount of settlement will be in excess of one hundred and seventy million dollars (U.S.) (approximately 70 million pounds) – this for one antibiotic drug alone, and this amount represents the over-pricing on that one drug only.

We are dealing here with numbers that befuddle. They do not indicate the monies that may accrue to the astute operators of the multinational drug companies. Add to this amount the profit of the sales of other drugs in the United States and other countries, and the amounts become too astronomical for the average mind to comprehend.

It is also important to consider the social costs of these actions to control drug prices. Someone must pay these costs. They include not only more than one hundred million dollars but unstated costs: the use of professional time, the use of the courts, the preparation of arguments, the recording and filing of evidence, and so on. These are expensive resources in any society. In addition, the clogging of the courts for such industrial highjinks somehow leaves one unamused.

And yet, under current systems of manufacture and distribution of prescription drugs, there is no way, other than highly expensive court action, to control the otherwise uncontrollable pricing of a market released from the usual competitive factors of a so-called free-market economy. Competition is the factor which prevents arbitrary pricing in a free market. This kind of competition does not prevail in drug manufacturing, except to a very minor and unimportant degree. The manufacture of drugs is a highly complex, highly sophisticated activity. By no means can it be performed by a cottage industry. It demands expensive research for the discovery of the newer and the better. Government controls, while essential to provide a degree of safety to the ill – a degree that can never be absolute – carry with them a price tag as well. The more rigid the controls, the more complete and exhaustive the laboratory and clinical trials before a release for general use, the greater the escalation of cost.

The more aggressive the search for the newer and the better, the more rapid the spiralling of cost. A new drug 'B' that pene-

trates the market before the older drug 'A' has had any opportunity to pay off its research, production and distribution costs,
will mean a very steep increase in the price of new drug 'B'; for
drug 'B' must now earn not only its own costs, but must redeem in
its price structure the losses incurred by the too early obsolescence
of drug 'A' – the one it has displaced. Under prevailing methods
of drug manufacture the search for the same drug may be carried
on in secrecy in several research centres, each belonging to different companies. The wastage in effort, the wastage in research
skills, that could be better employed than in unwittingly repro-
ducing work done elsewhere, the wastage in tooling production
assembly lines, that are needlessly repetitive, is beyond rational
estimation. But that it is considerable, there can be no doubt.
Add to these the substantial cost of distribution and aggressive
advertising and the price of the pill escalates.

There are two side effects from this kind of economic activity.
Firstly, the methods outlined above effectively eliminate the small
operator. The investment of capital in such an industry is pro-
hibitive other than to an industrial giant. No corner chemist can
possibly get into this game; it is only for the industrial colossus.

In order to destroy troublesome price competition the large
companies frequently develop the two-price structure in some
market areas. Whenever a small competitive firm tries to penetrate
the market, it may possibly succeed, providing its price is substantially lower than the price of the product manufactured by the
large corporation. In order to wipe out this kind of nuisance competition effectively the larger corporation retains its own price
for its own named product but puts on the market, in addition,
the identical product under another trade name, with a price that
seriously undercuts the price of the smaller competitor. The inevitable then happens. The small competitor in a short time is
wiped out by the outrageously low price of the larger manufacturer. When this is accomplished the second product with the
artificially very-low price also disappears and the major company
is left with its own product without any competition whatever.

Secondly, giants because of their size can only be few. They
don't knock each other in the games they play. To a very real
degree they need each other. They can parcel out world markets

among themselves – they can set prices that will give a satisfactory return without clobbering each other by 'free-market competition'. The giant is thus free from disastrous competition. The taxpayer, the consumer (the ill, who must buy drugs as prescribed by their doctors), it is these who pay the price, set in a market without traditional free-market competition.

It is difficult to see how the tetracycline settlement will do anything to reduce costs to the consumer. Indeed it will almost certainly have the reverse effect. Corporations, in this case the manufacturing drug giants, are bound to recover the losses of today's operations by adequate increases in tomorrow's price. But since this civil action was settled out of court there is no deterrent for the giants to engage again in the management of price to avoid competition. Indeed there is no assurance that the same kind of price fixing is not being conducted for other drugs at this moment. The giants can afford to take a calculated chance, if the only risk is civil-court action that must be initiated by individuals or by legal firms. Occasionally one or two such actions will erupt and, if the past is any indication, they will be settled by out-of-court settlements. The pricing system as it exists will go on unimpaired, and profits will continue to flow at whatever level is accepted as 'reasonable' by an industrial bureaucracy with its own special goals.

Queen Valium

Another attempt to recover excessive profits was made by a government. The British Government under the conditions of the National Health Insurance Act provides the ill with prescription drugs for a small 'deterrent' fee. The cost of the drug plus the fee of the dispensing pharmaceutical chemist is borne by the Government, paid for out of Government revenues.

By compliant response to vigorous aggressive promotion, doctors have made Valium the most frequently prescribed mood-affecting drug in history. Acting upon suggestions and some evidence that the price extracted from the United Kingdom Government by Hoffman La Roche (the Swiss manufacturers of

Valium) was excessive, the Government demanded that Roche justify its price on the basis of its costs. In the hearings between the Minister of Health and Roche, Government Representatives asked that the Roche Corporation present its accounting books for examination by Government-appointed auditors.

Roche flatly refused. As a Swiss Company and according to Swiss Law the refusal was legitimate. The Swiss Government has extensive legislation protecting secrecy in financial matters. However, by way of placating the United Kingdom Government, Roche offered to return to the Treasury a part of its profit on Valium, 'without prejudice' (legal jargon for saying 'we admit nothing and we establish no precedent').

Two significant conclusions can be drawn from this experience.

1. The real admission of over-pricing.

2. The difficulty which the British Government encountered in its attempt to force a manufacturer (from whom it purchases millions of pounds worth of pharmaceuticals) to justify its pricing method by an audit of its books. In its tough posture towards the British Government Roche was silently supported by the Swiss Government, the legitimate guardian of Roche. The Swiss Government is well known and well respected for its protective mantle towards financial operations generally and to the international corporation specifically.

A curious situation prevails when a sovereign government is being taken into court by an international corporation, as Roche has done with the British Government. The Government's request for a reduction in the price of Valium will reduce Roche's income by approximately four million pounds a year. The company claims it requires the higher amount in order to finance its admittedly high research costs (about one hundred million pounds a year).

Professor A. Hurliman, Roche's deputy research director, says 'If tranquilizer profits come down considerably all over the world, we would have to cut research.'   The question screams to be asked : if a powerful company exacts its own assessment for 'research costs' out of a sovereign government, who is doing what to whom? Is the company assessing its own private 'tax' for research? Or are governments and individual purchasers of drugs being taxed by international drug companies for research, with no accountability; without the presentation of a pretax budget?

In considering over-prescribing, Valium is a good illustrative drug for several reasons. Firstly, the enormity of its sales is an indication of the amount of psychotropic or mood-altering drugs being consumed in our time. Secondly, the mammoth sale indicates the success that can be confidently expected from skilful promotion of a drug to the profession. The promotion includes a constant level of direct mail or medical journal advertising, endless supplies of free samples to doctors and intensive and repeated detailing on a personal basis to each doctor by company representatives. The promotion also includes the free provision of Valium to hospital pharmacies, so that residents and interns – young doctors at the threshold of their prescribing career – become indoctrinated in the use of this drug while pursuing the hospital part of their training. The young doctor who has never prescribed Valium for his patients while continuing his training in hospital must be rare. This effectively shuts off any knowledge and experience he might acquire about other drugs that have a similar tranquillizing effect and have been accepted for many years prior to the arrival of Valium. This artificial creation of obsolescence of other useful drugs having similar physiological effect is especially important, because the doctor will never know that in most cases where Valium is prescribed there are other drugs as effective and less costly.

Thalidomide – The Low Point

Another attempt to balance the scale in the unequal struggle between the helpless buyer and the all-powerful manufacturer was the effort to compensate those harmed by a prematurely marketed drug – thalidomide. There were catastrophic defects in new-born babies, when mothers were prescribed this drug by doctors with simple faith in the statements of reputable, ethical drug manufacturers. Distillers Corporation proceeded to market thalidomide in the United Kingdom at a time when that drug was already under investigation in Germany and at a time when its sale was being withheld by the United States Government.

Hindsight gives a distinct advantage in apportioning responsibility for this decision made by the directors of Distillers Corporation. Needless to say, it was a decision they must now wish had never been made. Corporations – even highly successful multimillion ones – are, like mortals, fallible. Perhaps in situations where profit is a drive, if not an out-and-out goal, corporations may be even more fallible than humans. In fairness to Distillers, it should be stated that they proceeded with the sale of thalidomide only after it was approved for widespread dispensing by the appropriate department of the British Government, established to sanction drugs for dispensary sale.

For the 342 children in the United Kingdom forever maimed by thalidomide, actuaries have estimated that it will require 135 thousand pounds to maintain each child for its expected lifetime. This amounts to the not inconsiderable total of about four and a half million pounds. The law however is well established and clear. The manufacturer and distributor are responsible for the safety of their product.

Upon this principle a group of parents, acting on behalf of their children, took legal action against Distillers to compensate them for the calamitous cost of maintaining these crippled individuals for their lifetime. The twists and turns of this tortured action against Distillers Corporation will provide research material for years to come: to legal philosophers, to economists, to sociologists, to students of corporate power, to physicians, pharmacists, journalists and, one hopes, to legislators.

The block to a fair settlement was a legal one and no blame can fairly be thrown on Distillers Corporation. Within the area of law a company bears legal responsibilities to three 'publics' – the consumers, the employees, and the shareholders. It can be held to legal account by any of the three. To the consuming public it is liable for an infraction leading to the production and sale of a harmful product. To its employees it must, on pain of legal sanctions, provide safe working conditions and must observe its contractual obligations in industrial–labour agreements. But a company has an overriding responsibility to its shareholders, and a board of directors must exercise prudence in safeguarding the shareholders' financial interest. In other words, a Board is in difficulties in settling financial claims which may be at the shareholders' expense.

It was this last consideration that created the legal impasse blocking a settlement by the Board of Distillers towards the victims of the thalidomide tragedy. This impasse was finally broken by the courageous action of the editor of the London *Sunday Times* in risking a contempt action by the Attorney-General by publishing a series of articles highly critical of Distillers Corporation while litigation was still pending.

In commenting on the action of the *Sunday Times* editor, the judge, Lord Widgery, stated: 'This seems to us to make it perfectly clear that the intention behind publication is that public opinion should be aroused on this issue, and that as a result of such public opinion the children may obtain better terms than would otherwise be available to them.'

Although the *Sunday Times* was found guilty of Contempt of Court, this was indeed the effect of the articles. Not only was the public aroused, but influential shareholders themselves brought pressure on the Board to proceed quickly towards a fairer settlement than had previously been proposed. Thus, when all these pieces in the legal jigsaw were put together; when the *Sunday Times* published its editorials in legalistic contempt but in moral rightness; when parents were determined to sacrifice all of their worldly possessions in pursuit of a fair settlement; when a significant number of institutional shareholders came to hold the view that the corporation should settle; and when the Board itself was urged by its ordinary shareholders to effect a settlement – only then was progress towards a fair settlement started.

5 Patents: The Names of the Games

The growth of the drug industry follows curiously the story of Jack Horner. He, it will be recalled, forever sat in his corner concocting his puddings and pies. And then, for mysterious and as yet unexplained reasons, he stuck in his thumb and, lo and behold, pulled out a plum and said, 'what a good boy am I'.

For centuries corner apothecaries, the forerunners of the drug industry, went about making their secret concoctions, and sold them as remedies. Secrecy was what protected their enterprise and their genius. Then suddenly out popped a plum: the notion of patents. Patents were made legitimate by nearly all nations. Now the prevention of copying a secret formula no longer depended upon cloak-and-dagger methods passed on from father to son. With patents, copying became illegal with all the force and apparatus of the law: police, courts, fines or imprisonments, in order to protect the product from illegitimate copying.

Patents on drugs evolved, not from anything within the nature and development of science, but out of the ideas underlying commercial relationships. Indeed the notion of a patent and of the secrecy that is involved – of a restriction upon the flow of ideas – has always been and still is foreign to the ethos of science and held suspect by nearly all scientists. Secrecy is diametrically opposed to science. Science and, within it, scientific discovery and research, depends upon the free, unfettered flow of information and ideas. Traditionally, scientific research requires the publication of all details, conferences with free exchange of ideas, and critical, sometimes acrimonious, comment.

Without this climate of complete freedom of disclosure, the major scientific discoveries that have so completely altered our way of life could never take place. Scientists freely borrow from each other: ideas, methods, technology, even end-products. If

Enders had patented, instead of freely published, his discovery of a method of growing viruses, Salk probably would never have discovered his vaccine that has prevented untold thousands from developing poliomyelitis. Leaf through any scientific or medical journal today and you will read open accounts of new procedures in surgery and new concepts regarding the diagnosis or treatment of diseases, completely free from patent. You will also see the reports of trials of new drugs produced by the drug industry, most of them patented.

The tendency to protection, either by patent or by secrecy, is most prevalent in those scientific areas close to industrial goals or allied to war. In industry profit is protected by patents. In war it is national security that is protected by secrecy. For certain scientific discoveries and methods, the classification as secret, deemed essential for national security, is perhaps justified, given the current state of our civilization. There is less justification for the maintenance of patents for drugs for the protection of profits for industry.

The area of patents is highly complex, shrouded in legal jargon, subject to change from day to day and from country to country. It provides a rich mine for the workings of legal gurus, so highly specialized that it is rare to find the average lawyer willing to handle a case where patent infringement is involved, without seeking the opinion of expert counsel in the field. Patent laws are enshrined in formidable documents with amendments, legal opinions and courtly dicta, with innumerable exceptions, and are surrounded by court actions that run on for years and years.

Curiously, while tedious and prolonged court actions are taking place between adversary firms about patents, these same drug firms, who oppose each other in the jungle war of patent infringement, meet in leather-chaired club rooms for agreement to fix a price.

To further confuse the picture for the reader, and creating further bonanzas for patent lawyers, court actions take place, concerned with applications of firms who wish legally to infringe on existing patents. And, to top this legal hodgepodge, court actions are pursued against those who have already been granted patents on the basis of misinformation.

But the central point about patent protection for drugs is sharp and crystal clear – profit for the industry. It has little else to be said for it. The tiny kernel of truth about patent protection for drugs is reward for the inventor. The argument runs something like this. If you have a property – say a house – you are granted right of sole possession by the law. In legal terms your capital in this possession is deemed to be yours. You may rent this house and receive rental revenues as long as your sole possession of the capital remains protected by law.

Inventors or discoverers of new drugs can, by analogy and by fairness, be considered to have their investment in intellectual capital, embodied in their formula of the drug or in their method of producing it. Just as the individual owning the house has invested his money (capital) into the house, so the man who has invested his knowledge, his ingenuity and his time has an investment in intellectual capital that deserves some kind of statutory protection. Just as the man who has used his knowledge, skill and time to write a book is entitled to whatever fruits the copyright may bring, so the one who has discovered the drug is entitled to a rental or a royalty or a purchase price for that invention. Thus patents were originally designed to protect and compensate for intellectual capital.

But like other fine, intellectually designed economic models this one just hasn't worked out. That is not to say that some inventors have not profited. But the working model represented by patents on drugs has failed in several respects, each of them important to society.

Firstly, it is rare for any individual to hold a new drug patent. Most researchers in the area of new drugs are members of research teams working for firms and the firm takes out the patent in its own name. 'New drugs', as defined by companies in the drug industry, may also be the result of molecular manipulations or combinations of already existing drugs, as we have seen. Nevertheless, responding to the bureaucratic spur, teams of researchers are assigned to creating such new drugs. Many such problems require considerable resources of money and brain. In these areas there is rarely an individual inventor. Where certain members of the team consistently shine in inventiveness, the company in its own interest sees that these individuals are rewarded to keep them from moving to a competitor.

The result is that the overwhelming majority of patents on new drugs are held by the larger multinational firms. This can be called intellectual capital of a sort. But by moving it from its intended goal of an 'intellect' to a firm it becomes inseparable from plain and ordinary capital.

The industry replies that, if there were no protection afforded to firms by reason of patents, they could not continue with their research programme for new drugs. A firm penetrating the market with a new drug, representing a formidable investment in research, would find its market almost immediately destroyed by a number of copiers who could duplicate the drug. The copying firms, having no research costs, could easily undersell the innovating firm. The spokesmen for the drug industry insist this would mean – 'no new drugs'.

The facts do not support them. 'New drugs' are not really new. They are the staging points on an endless road of discovery. No one really invents a new drug. New drugs evolve, and the particular scientist, with special knowledge and the 'hunch', who happens to live and work at the right moment when all the previous discoveries make the timing right – he makes the discovery. It is significant that, not infrequently, another scientist in another laboratory in another part of the world makes the same discovery entirely independently. All discoverers in science stand on the shoulders of those who have gone before. Every true scientist acknowledges this heritage. It was only when corporate interest became dominant that the right of a party claiming a patent for the discovery became prominent. Patents serve the industry much more than the individual discoverer and certainly much more than society.

A Senate investigation (United States) disclosed these facts regarding the protection of patents: Italy for many years had no patent protection for drugs. There is no evidence whatsoever that the death rates or sickness rates among Italians were higher than with other national groups. Belgium, Panama and the United States were more diligent than any other nations in rigorously protecting patent holders in drugs; there is no evidence that the

rate of discovery of new drugs in these three countries was significantly improved as a result of this. On the other hand studies
showed that the discovery of new drugs in countries without
patent protection was ten times higher than discoveries in countries protected by patent laws. The conclusion would appear to be
warranted that in this industry the mere existence of patent protection is not a guarantee of invention nor its absence much of a
barrier.

So much for patent protection being a spur to invention of new
drugs.

Another difficulty created by the retention of patent laws in
the interest of the drug industry is the smoke screen of names in
order to protect patent territory. To protect your patented product against invaders you identify your product by a patented
name.

An upstart firm may make something close to your product –
indeed, on the basis of pharmaceutical effect, identical with your
product – but they must not use your name. If your product is
patented with the name 'gloop', gloop it is – not 'whiz' nor 'duz'
nor a myriad of other names. Furthermore you may license other
firms to make gloop and receive a royalty on every parcel of gloop
that is sold by them, but they must not use the name gloop. In
order that profits can come to your firm from competitors they
cannot dislodge you from the advantages of your heavily
promoted gloop.

As an example of the confusion that may be created by a patent
name, the drug thalidomide (the patent held by Chemie Grünenthal of West Germany) was identified, either by the parent firm
or by licensing or other trade arrangements, as a single drug or in
combination with other drugs under the following names: *

Algosediv – 50 mg. combination with acetylsalicylic acid in tabs.; also
   12·5 mg. combination with A P C in suppositories (Chemie Grünenthal, West Germany)
Asmaval – 12·5 mg. combination with ephedrin HCl in tab. (The
   Distillers Co. Ltd, Great Britain)

* Sjöström, H. and Nilsson, R. *Thalidomide and the Power of the Drug
Companies*, Penguin Books, 1972, p. 39.

Contergan – 25 mg. tabs.; syrup containing 50 mg./teaspoon; 100 mg. suppositories. (Chemie Grünenthal, West Germany)

Contergan Forte – 100 mg. tabs. (Chemie Grünenthal, West Germany)

Distaval – 25 mg. tabs. (The Distillers Co. Ltd, Great Britain)

Distaval Forte – 100 mg. tabs. (The Distillers Co. Ltd, Great Britain)

Grippex – 12·5 mg. combination with quinine, ascorbic acid, phenacetin and Salicylamide capsules. (Chemie Grünenthal, West Germany)

Kevadon – 100 mg. tabs. (William S. Merrell Co. Ltd, Canada)

Neurosedyn – 25 mg. and 100 mg. tabs. (Astra, Sweden)

Peracon-Expectorans – 40 mg. combination with ipecac dragees; also liquid. (Kali-Chemie AG, West Germany)

Softenon – 25 mg. tabs. (Chemie Grünenthal, West Germany)

Softenon Forte – 100 mg. tabs. (Chemie Grünenthal, West Germany)

Talimol – 100 mg. tabs. (Frank W. Horner Co. Ltd, Canada)

Tensival – 12·5 mg. combination with hydrachlorothiazide tabs. (The Distillers Co. Ltd, Great Britain)

Valgis – 50 mg. combination with acetylsalicylic acid and phenacetin tabs. (The Distillers Co. Ltd, Great Britain)

Valgraine – 12·5 mg. combination with ergotamine tartrate tabs. (The Distillers Co. Ltd, Great Britain)

Calmorex – 25 mg. tabs. (Laboratorio FRC, Italy)

Enterosediv – 10 mg. tabs. combination with bacitracin, dihydro-streptomycin, pantothenate and diiodohydroxyquinoline (Chemie Grünenthal, Switzerland)

Gastrimide – 50 mg. tabs. combination with triethyl (4-stilbenehy-droxyethyl) ammonium chloride (LIVSA, Milan, Italy)

Imida-Lab – 50 mg. tabs. (Laboratories Lab, Lisbon, Portugal)

Imidan – 50 mg. tabs. (Lab.Peyta, Spain)

Imidene – 50 mg. tabs. (Smit, Torino, Italy)

Imidene Ipnotico – 50 mg. tabs. combination with allylmethylbutyl barbiturate (Smit, Torino, Italy)

Lulamin – name given by Nordiske Pharmakope; no manufacturer given

Noctosediv – 25 mg. tabs. combination with secobarbital (Chemie Grünenthal, Switzerland)

Noxodyn – 40 mg. tabs. and suppositories, combination with pento-barbital (Astra, Sweden)

Pantosediv – (Chemie Grünenthal, West Germany)

Prednisediv – 5 mg. capsules, combination with prednisolone, salicyl-amide, aminopyrine, ascorbic acid and aluminium hydroxide

(Chemie Grünenthal, West Germany)

Profarmil – 25 mg. regular tabs. 50 mg. strong tabs. and 10 mg. pediatric tabs. (Profarmi, Milan, Italy)

Quetimid – 50 mg. tabs. (Biocorfa, Milan, Italy)

Quietoplex – 50 mg. tabs. (LIVSA, Milan, Italy)

Sedalis – name given by Arzneimittel-Forsch, no manufacturer given

Sedi-Lab – 50 mg. tabs. (Laboratories Lab, Lisbon, Portugal)

Sedimide – 50 mg. tabs. and 150 mg, suppositories (Mugolio Soc. Acc., Italy)

Sedoval K-17 – 50 mg. tabs. (Italfarma, Torino, Italy)

Theophyl-choline – 20 mg. tabs. combination with theophylline and choline (Perkins Chemical Co., Italy)

Ulcerfen – 20 mg. tabs. combination with hydroxyphenylcyclamine chloride (Biocorfa, Milan, Italy)

Thirty-seven names for drugs in which thalidomide was the sole or the active agent! There is no doubt that if sales of thalidomide had not been aborted, and taking into consideration the aggressiveness of the promotion associated with thalidomide, the spread of the product by world-wide trade arrangements would have resulted in several hundred more names, all of them protected by patent and all the names having no similarity to the word 'thalidomide' whatsoever.

It is the glut of names that ensures a profit for the company holding the patent on the product. It is a part of the same babel of names that confuse, boggle, obfuscate, harry and irritate the life of a physician. There is a limit to memory. When there are thirty-seven names for one drug, whenever you want to recall a single one in order to write it down on a prescription pad, the name of the one that you write is the one that you have most recently seen or heard. Again, the company with the promotional muscle is the one that will win the prescription pad.

A wise teacher in therapeutics said: 'If you tell a student the name of one drug for a specific disease, he will remember it – if you tell him a dozen he will forget them all.' By a plethora of names the drug industry assures that the only one the doctor remembers is the last one he has just read or heard. It is the task of sophisticated and skilful promoters of the drug company, armed with a nearly unlimited budget, to make sure that the last name the doctor hears echoing forever is the patented 'gloop'. For patented read profitable.

Another effect of patents in the drug industry has been the phenomenal growth and success of the multinational corporation. In probably no other industrial endeavour is there such a high proportion of multinational conglomerates. Securely protected in pricing by international agreements that exist either in official documents or by tacit understanding, firms could develop either production or distribution facilities in many countries. This has the effect of eliminating the small firm that might start in individual countries.

In important respects, in failure to encourage discovery, in creating confusion about drugs among doctors, and by the power of multinationals to operate legitimately and avoid price competition, patent protection for the drug industry has outlived its usefulness in the public interest.

6 The Costs of Feeling Better

In the general marketing area, where supply and demand can be estimated with some degree of accuracy, meaningful calculations and planning may be done to curb the foreseeable demand. If, for example, there is a limit to the supply of energy, we may be able to trim demand to meet the limited supply. Pockets of waste can be searched out and possibly eliminated. Voluntarily or by decree we can drive smaller cars. We can reduce wasteful use of our resources. Such things may be done without seriously impairing standards of living and with only unimportant changes in life style. In addition, deficiencies in supply act as a stimulus leading towards a solution in the long run. To use again the comparison of the energy crisis, the availability of alternative energy resources is given prime consideration. This stimulus to rational activity, created by a shortage of supply within the energy system, provides sharp contrast to any conceivable limits to the supply of pills hindering the drug industry.

Indeed, the most serious single defect in the health system lies in the danger of an unlimited supply of drugs to fill an unlimited demand, or a demand that can be manipulated to be limitless.*

It is not possible to predict in any rational way the demand for drugs. Theoretically the largest part of the demand has to do with the treatment of disease. Some areas of disease are definable. We can get reasonably accurate figures regarding the total amount of cancer, diabetes, heart attacks, strokes, high blood pressure, mental disease, and so on from morbidity tables issued by insurance companies and from government statistical bureaux. From

* 'The Roche affair was by no means the first indication that these drugs are being over-prescribed in Britain. And in the U.S.A. Diazepam (Valium) prescriptions are increasing by seven million annually. At this rate the arrival of the Millenium would coincide with the total tranquillization of America.' Editorial, *Lancet*, 19 May 1973, p. 1101.

these figures we may develop some estimate of the enormity of the problem facing researchers for new drugs to meet demand for treatment. We may even go further. We may determine the proportion of research that should be devoted to basic research (concentrated upon new information having to do with the chemistry and biology of the individual cell itself) and how much to mission-orientated research – the kind of research that results in a specific treatment. By and large it is in the enormously important basic research where the real gains in treatment of disease have been made, and where the promise of advance in the future is greatest.

But from the point of view of the drug industry this is not the most productive area. For industry the important area is where profits are greatest. The more pills sold, the better. This is not to condemn the drug industry but merely to place it squarely in line with industrial goals that are universally accepted and respected. The drug industry is neither more nor less noble than any other large corporate area. The following are two personal expressions of the responsibility of business to society. The first (1964) is by Mr David Rockefeller,* President of Chase Manhattan Bank:

A creative management philosophy must be one which not only seeks through efficient operation to maximize profit but which also recognizes its responsibility to render economic service – service by private-enterprise to the public interest. The British statesman, Lord Halifax, liked to define services as 'the rent we pay for our room on earth'. In the case of business enterprises, this rent comes due, not once a month but every day of the year. We can pay it by contributing through creative management to making this a better and more prosperous world for all mankind.

The second is by Mr Arnold Maremont * – who runs his own corporation – at a meeting of the National Conference Board (United States) 1964:

Let's not confuse the company managers in their role as managers, with their role as individuals. A Company man, in a social responsibility sense, is not a man at all. He is just two dimensions and he is not human. Since a corporation has no conscience and is not a per-

* Eels, R. and Walton, C., *Conceptual Foundations of Business*, Richard D. Irwin Inc., Illinois, 1969, p. 213.

son, it cannot be charitable. It cannot take shareholders' profits to help mankind, womankind or even the animal world.

These are apparently divergent views but divergent in semantics only. Both agree that profit is the primary goal – one bluntly, one elegantly.

If concepts having to do with the terms 'supply' and 'demand' differ radically in the drug industry from other industries, it is because of the nature of 'dis-ease' and not from any significant difference in the personalities or goals or social conscience of the industrial bureaucracy. It is possible to estimate what the energy needs may be in the foreseeable future for any household or for any individual. It is not possible to make any such predictable limit for drug needs. It is not possible to make predictions for the needs or demands for that group of drugs, immensely important to the industry, that generally speaking are designed, promoted, and sold to make you 'feel better'.

If anyone wishes to see an example of endless variations on the theme of the urge to 'feel better', look at any privately owned television network for the duration of any programme. Have you a cold? Do you feel stuffed up? Congested? Rotten? Depressed? Tired? Sleepless? Sleepy? Lack pep? Frantic? Worried? Old? Constipated? etcetera – 'You can feel better.'

Thus a form of brainwashing becomes effective. Listen to the howls of rage, if any suggestion is made to curtail the advertising of drugs. A horde of waspish experts in public relations, sophisticated in the ways of mass persuasion, is let loose. Newspaper publishers, radio and television executives, paper manufacturers, the printing industry, the wholesale and retail drug industry and of course the all-powerful multinational in drug manufacturing – all stiffen at any suggestion of criticism of advertising. And supporting these powerful interests would be those millions who have already been well brainwashed to believe that they cannot possibly ever get better from feeling rotten, if the public media keep silent about drugs.

The dimension of the totality of feeling rotten is enormous, expanding and incalculable. This creates limitless demand, something that gives the drug industry a unique advantage over any other. There must be an upper limit of the demand for cars, wheat, soap, peanuts, energy and so on, which is calculable. Not so with the demand to feel better – an indefinable and limitless demand that reaches into infinity. There is a transiency and even an unreality to merely 'feeling good', especially when compared to 'feeling better'.

The analysis of the demand for drugs to feel better is complex. Is it life style? Is it rising expectations? Is it a Freudian wish to get back to the womb? But there is no doubt that the demand to feel better is growing and so is the sale of drugs, legal as well is illicit. Indeed, there is a relationship between the sale of banned drugs on the black market and the sale of legitimate drugs over-the-counter and by prescription. Are youngsters conditioned by their elders' pill popping? Or are they conditioned by some paediatricians and practitioners who write prescriptions for everything? Or are we all influenced by television viewing, with impressive pictures showing the medication zoom directly to the very spot on the exact organ that is causing the feeling of 'dis-ease'?

Are the lesser developed countries climbing into the areas of feeling better as well? The drug-manufacturing industry has become more and more active in promoting sales in the poorer countries. And the sales to the poorer countries have resulted in higher profits than the equivalent sales of the same drugs to developed countries.

The price for tetracycline in Europe was twenty-eight dollars per kilogram. At the same time in India it was one hundred and thirteen dollars. Prednisone for Europeans was five hundred and fifty dollars per kilo: one thousand five hundred and ninety-three dollars to the Indians. Vitamin C was two dollars and forty cents per one hundred in Europe: nine dollars and seventy cents in India. Generally speaking prices in India were three hundred and fifty-seven per cent higher than the average European price.*

How much does the growing sale of drugs in developing countries represent real need and how much the demand for feeling

* A U.S. Congressional Study quoted by Levinson C., 'The Multinational Pharmaceutical Industry', published by the International Federation of Chemical and General Workers Unions, 1972, p. 69.

better? This is anyone's guess. It is fair to assume that in the demand for goods the developing countries are moving along the ways of western conventional wisdom. The goodies of the West today become the goodies of the East tomorrow. And nowhere is this more likely to be true than in the cherished goal of health. The result of all these factors is a growing system that is intended to provide all the things deemed necessary for 'health' (western style) and with no limit to its growth.

The inputs into this system take enormous and ever increasing amounts of scarce human and physical resources. Rare chemicals, sophisticated production equipment, plant, packaging, transportation, highly skilled personnel and research workers, hospitals, technicians, nurses and doctors are all integral parts of this system. The modern drug industry, although a relative newcomer into the system, has achieved a position of dominance, replacing the medical profession. The drug industry now determines the volume and, what is more important, the direction of research for this system. Furthermore, the drug industry has added a new and non-essential factor to this system: the element of aggressive promotion in the sale of drugs.

Several subsidiary questions arise before we can attempt to determine the price of feeling better. One has to do with the nature and cost of industrially directed research. Research by industry has already been considered and was found to be enormous and mainly directed towards industrial goals. It is research primarily orientated towards increasing sales, into producing 'me too' and combination drugs for the purpose of maintaining a high level of productivity of the same drug and to preventing sales decline due to trade-name obsolescence.

But ultimately we must deal with the thorny question of priorities. How much for drugs? How much for other systems that help to determine the quality of life: education, food, energy, transportation, housing, etcetera?

A large slice of society's contribution to research is converted into the special kind of research of the drug industry. This flow of research funds, extracted from the consumer, is derived from drug sales. This flow and its expenditure is controlled by the drug industry. It is inevitable that this flow be directed towards research in line with industrial goals. We cannot have it both ways. We cannot have both the brand new pill that will make us feel better when we are in the dumps and have the cancer research – all for the same dollar. It is one or the other – not both.

In this way there is a pyramiding effect on the growth of industrially promoted drug research controlled by sales management. The inspired scientist, squeezed out of basic research by lack of funds, not welcomed into university-controlled basic research, joins the bustling industrial research team. The consumer – the patient – is cheated in two ways. He is forced to pay a tax for a kind of research that is directed towards the new model to replace the old, and that diverts his money away from essential basic research. Furthermore, he must pay the heavy cost incurred by industrial promotion to convince his doctor that this new model pill will make him really feel better. He has no choice.

7 The Battle of Septra-Septrim AD 1973

To illustrate some of the events that involve the industrial medical complex, an examination of the introduction and promotion of a new drug named Septra (United States) and Septrim (United Kingdom) may be informative.

In 1973 Septra – 'the aggressive antibacterial' – was introduced into the prescription market in the United States and Canada by Burroughs Wellcome and Company.

In 1959 a group of Professors in United States medical schools initiated an advisory letter called the *Medical Letter*. Its aim was to provide practising physicians with information regarding new drugs without advertising and other promotional influence.

In 1972 the Provincial Government of Manitoba in Canada established (on the basis of one of the recommendations of a Provincial Commission, studying the pricing and marketing of prescription drugs) a continuing committee of drug experts to advise on Drug Standards and Therapeutics.

These three formed the *dramatis personae* of a battle that was joined between on the one hand Burroughs Wellcome and, on the other hand, the editors of the *Medical Letter* and the *Bulletin of the Manitoba Drug Standards and Therapeutics Committee*.

Burroughs Wellcome was the industrial protagonist in this contest, along with a financially interested associate – the giant Roche firm. Roche marketed the same product under the label 'Bactrim'. The choice of Burroughs Wellcome as an example of marketing aggression is not capricious nor arbitrary. Burroughs Wellcome is selected because it is the firm generally regarded by the medical profession as the most 'ethical of the ethicals'. From its historical beginning Burroughs Wellcome has earned and rightly deserved this recognition. There are no public shareholders in this firm and all the profits from Burroughs Wellcome are devoted to the research of the Wellcome Research Institute. With this kind of altruistic background it is not surprising that the promotional sales policy of Burroughs Wellcome was low keyed and dignified and, because of its low profile, the firm represented integrity and reliability in the drug industry to many within the medical profession.

But this kind of sales policy, laid down by the character of the founder, could not withstand the relentless and inescapable surge of modern marketing. The evolution of the modern corporation represents a change from owner-directed to a board of directors and, finally, to sales orientation by a management bureaucracy. In a variety of fields more than one large firm has disappeared, because it failed to move with its competitors and develop the changes demanded by modern aggressive marketing.

In spite of the zeal that modern drug companies showed in beaming the message of obsolescence and frequently introducing new drugs, Burroughs Wellcome maintained its leisurely pedestrian pace in developing and promoting dependable pharmaceutical products. And then came Septra – the new model. Septra represents a turning point in the marketing policy of Burroughs Wellcome. According to objective reports in medical journals, this combination of a sulpha and antibiotic did offer some advantages in a proportion of bladder and kidney infections that had become resistant to other drugs. But how did Burroughs Wellcome project the image of Septra?

A number of conferences and trips for physicians occupying influential posts in universities and medical schools were arranged. One such conference held in Boston in 1972 collected from all parts of Canada and the United States several hundred doctors, all influential within the medical hierarchy.

Medical Associations rely for an essential part of their revenue upon the advertising in their journals. They also depend on the advertiser for financial support for their conventions. University departments rely, for a significant proportion of research grants, on the pharmaceutical industry. All these factors create a firm bond between the pharmaceutical industry and the agencies of the medical profession. An accepted alliance, the industrial–medical complex, has gradually become dominantly controlled by the industry.

In due time the flood of brochures starts being delivered to the doctor, the samples start arriving, the representatives and the detail men enter the door, and the market is made receptive by word of mouth and by discussions of the new drugs by influential members of the profession. The flow of information is from then on high. Some of it comes from the leaders of the profession who attend the conferences, even from the simple fact that spreads down among the residents and interns of the teaching centres that the chief participated in an important conference on Septra. These kinds of messages, in an orderly succession, hammer home the point. In every sense, in style, in paper, in words, in repetition, the glossies of the commercial artist, of the copywriter and of the master printer are indeed masterpieces of these crafts. They are beautifully produced, artfully worded, such a triumph of colour printing that even the sceptic is reluctant to deposit them in their ultimate destination – the dust bin. So the glossies achieve their intended goal and remain on the desk for several days or several weeks.

In this way Septra arrives into the doctor's life: 'a new kind of antibacterium'; 'the aggressive antibacterial', with a red arrow pointing straight through the heart of an ugly, hairy bacteria. Page two of the glossy says: 'The aggressive antibacterial in respiratory tract infections', and again there is the arrow through the heart of a bacteria, this one with less hair and not so ugly, but lying squarely inside the helplessly panting lung. On the lung page there are unequivocal statements such as,

a new kind of antibacterial, not a single entity, not a typical combination. Septra contains trimethoprim, a potent new antibacterial designed and discovered by Wellcome research, and sulfa-methoxazole in a ratio that achieved true antibacterial symmetry. Septra was specifically designed to block simultaneously two bacterial enzymes (both fatal for bacterial survial) and thus to act more decisively than either of the components used alone.

On the kidney page, printed in azure blue, red, purple, green and puce, there are two kidneys with their tubes running down to a white bladder. In the right kidney there is a particularly horrible bacterium with lots of long, scraggly hairs, but it, too, has its inners punched through by the double coloured Septra arrow. And down below, where lies the white bladder, there is another bacterium with fewer but thicker black hairs, and its heart is punctured by the two-toned Septra arrow. Here on this page the reading is: 'Aggressive antibacterial in urinary tract infections. Bactericidal against major urinary pathogens. With the exception of pseudomonas, Septra is active against major gram negative bacilli occurring in the urine: E. Coli, Klebsiella E. Aerogenes, P. Mirabilis, P. Vulgaris and S. Aureus and N. Gonorrhea.'

Other sections on this kidney and bladder page have paragraphs that read: 'High clinical success rate significant. Significant drug levels. With little likelihood of resistance. Rapid high urine levels.'

The last page of this four-page glossy has the upper half illustrated with an even bigger monster of a bacterium, stabbed by that multicoloured arrow right through its middle, and, in case you have forgotten by the time you arrive at page four, there is, in even bigger and redder letters,

SEPTRA DESTROYS THE PATHOGENS DISCOURAGES RESISTANCE

The other half of page four is devoted, in closely printed, much smaller type, to statements on contra-indications, precautions, adverse reactions, dosage and administration, dosage forms and twenty-two references from medical literature.

Another mailing is a smaller but somewhat similar glossy, of four pages, in addition to a stiff card with both sides repeating the message in question and answer form. This card contains a rip-off post card, addressed and stamped, inviting doctors to ask for additional information on Septra. This card, if sent, results in an elaborate multicoloured booklet, again profusely illustrated, all about Septra in twenty-four glossy pages. To this promotional assault must be added four-page spreads of coloured advertisements in many of the leading medical journals and calendars, and seemingly unlimited supplies of samples of Septra.

Only the blind, the deaf or the dead in the profession could have avoided receiving this barrage, with its message of something really splendid.

To counter this enormously expensive and sophisticated marketing onslaught two voices were heard.

In April 1972 the Government of the Province of Manitoba in Canada received a report from the Advisory Committee on Central Drug Purchasing and Distribution. This committee had been constituted by the Provincial Government a year previously. The terms of reference sought recommendations to reduce the price of drugs without reducing the quality. One of the recommendations the Government implemented was the establishment of a Committee of Drug Standards and Therapeutics, composed of recognized leaders in the pharmaceutical and medical professions with special knowledge and interest in drug quality and effectiveness.

By coincidence, the first report of the Manitoba Committee, in its simple two-page, unadorned, mimeographed letter to the Medical Profession of Manitoba, was distributed at about the time the promotional drive for Septra was in full swing. The contrast between this plain mimeographed letter and the glossies from Burroughs Wellcome is highly significant.

The following extracts are from this letter on Septra:

But during the years of its use overseas, resistance has emerged, especially among coliforms, and such resistance may be transferred from strain to strain. The occurrence of severe haematologic reaction, secondary to folate deficiency, points to specific interference with normal bone-marrow function.

In conclusion Septra is not the drug of first choice. For example in conditions such as gonorrhoea, most urinary tract infections and typhoid fever in which equally effective and less potentially toxic treatment is available in most cases.

It is of no value in the frequently met mycoplasma pneumoniae infections.

It should not be regarded as a broad spectrum anti-microbial agent for unselected general use.

The obvious and gross divergence between the claims by Burroughs Wellcome copywriters and the information in the simple low-profile two-page mimeographed letter from the Manitoba Drug Standards and Therapeutic Committee is sobering and even sinister in its implications.

The other voice heard from the other side of the Septra battle came from the prestigious medical publication, the *Medical Letter*. First published in a regular bi-weekly series, the *Medical Letter* carries no advertising whatever. Its single commitment is to the doctor who supports the *Medical Letter* by means of an annual subscription.

As the basis of its claim to impartiality, the following statement came from the first *Medical Letter* of 23 January 1959:

HOW DRUGS ARE EVALUATED

The decision to investigate a particular drug is based on such factors as the potential importance of the drug, the extent of its promotion and prescription, inquiries from physicians, and any special hazards that may attend the use of the drug. On the basis of his knowledge of the specific drug or of a related drug, a consultant is selected from among the broad panel of clinicians and investigators participating in the work of the *Medical Letter*. His task is to study the claims for the drug; to analyze the evidence of pharmacologic and clinic studies; to tap the knowledge of other clinicians and investigators; and to prepare a preliminary report on the drug in terms of effectiveness, known or likely adverse effects, and possible alternative medications.

The manufacturers are asked to supply material supporting the claims for the drug, and both published and available unpublished studies are carefully examined. Particular note is made of the results of controlled clinical trial; and the backgrounds of the individuals in the institutions participating in the trials are carefully considered. When the draft is received by the editorial board it is studied and discussed with other consultants. A revised draft is then prepared. This is submitted to the members of the editorial and advisory board of the *Medical Letter*, all of whom participated actively in the review of all drafts, and of other clinicians-investigators who have had special experience with the drug, or type of drug being used; the draft is also sent for review to the Medical Director of the Pharmaceutical Company producing the drug.

Many criticisms, suggestions and questions come in from the reviewers by notes, letters and telephone calls. Usually, there is further extended communication by mail, phone and personal consultation, followed by final checking and editing to ensure that the appraisal not only is accurate in its facts and representative of the consensus of consultants, but is also easily readable by busy physicians. The resulting evaluation is published in the next available issue of the *Medical Letter*.

The *Medical Letter* has achieved a respected place as a reliable source of continuing education about drugs for the conscientious doctor. It had this to say about Septra:

Although sulfa-methoxazole-trimethoprim (Septra) has been used abroad for a variety of infections, the only indication approved by the Food and Drug Administration (United States) is for the treatment of chronic urinary tract infections due to susceptible organisms.

The combination is effective for this indication. As with most other anti-microbial drugs however (Septra) is likely to be successful when the infecting organisms are susceptible and likely to fail when they are resistant, whether the infection is chronic or not. In acute or chronic urinary tract infections, many *Medical Letter* Consultants prefer to use older drugs such as sulfonamides alone, ampicillin, or tetracycline, when the infecting organisms are susceptible to them.

Although not approved for such use by the F.D.A., sulfa-methoxazole-trimethoprim (Septra) is the drug of choice for patients with typhoid fever, resistant both to chloramphenicol and ampicillin.

Toxicity: trimethoprim (Septra) is a folate antagonist and many hematologic reactions to the combination have been reported; some *Medical Letter* Consultants believe that these are poorly documented, however and that serious hematologic reactions are rare.

Reports of serious nephrotoxicity (kidney damage) in patients with diminished renal function (S. Kalowski, *Lancet*, 1:394, 1973) indicate a need for caution, especially since many patients with chronic urinary tract infections already have some loss of renal function. Until the effect on renal function is clarified, it would be prudent not to use this combination in patients with a serum creatinine above 2 mg-100 ml and to reserve its use in any patient with diminished renal function for urinary infections that are resistant to other anti-microbial agents (*Medical Letter* hand book of antimicrobial therapy, 21 January 1972, p. 42).

CONCLUSION: The combination of trimethoprim and sulfa-methoxazole (Bactrim-Roche; Septra-Burroughs Wellcome) is now available for treatment of chronic urinary tract infection. This combination is effective in urinary tract infections, but in patients with diminished renal function other microbial drugs may be safer. One hundred tablets of Bactrim or Septra generally cost the patients between thirty and forty dollars, compared with about three dollars for generic sulfonamides.

This contrast between the language of claims by the manufacturer and the statements by professional observers is a serious matter. Clearly both the cost of drugs and the health of the consumer are at issue.

The effect on the price of drugs is obvious. The costs of this promotional material in the mails; the cost of unlimited supplies of samples; the cost of conferences attended by members of the profession; the cost of advertising in medical journals: all these can be reclaimed only by the price structure of the drug.

The effect on health can be even more serious. If a new drug is widely used for conditions for which there is no agreement among the experts, and with as yet undisclosed adverse effects, instead of an older, equally effective drug with a longer history of relatively safe use, it is the patient who pays in added suffering, in increased costs, in time loss from work, perhaps in hospitalization.

Why the disagreement? Why the glaring difference between the statements of advertisers and the statement of experts? Who wins this battle of conflicting words?

There is little doubt who will win in the battle of Septra. The mimeographed letter from the Manitoba Drug Standards Therapeutics Committee and the *Medical Letter* are subdued monochromatic statements in contrast to the polychromatic glossies of Burroughs Wellcome.

These two professionally sponsored letters will reach and be read by approximately 5 per cent of practising physicians once only. The glossies about Septra-Septrim are aimed to reach every practising physician over and over again. The bombardment in the advertising pages of medical journals will continue. The supplies of samples will arrive again and again. The resistance, subdued, feeble and truthful, will be annihilated.

The Winners and the Losers

An ally in the force that might be exerted against the promotional barrage is government in its control of new drugs. It is assumed that governmental agencies, who control the release of new drugs, supervise statements of drug companies, judge them, perform independent tests, and only after the weighing of evidence *pro* and *con* permit the drug company to release new drugs for prescription sale. In this function, however, governments do as well as budgets allow and political reality permits. By their nature the budgets of government agencies must be limited, while the promotional budgets of drug multinational companies have demonstrably nearly unlimited dimension. Governments cannot recover costs of their information services, except out of budgetary allotment.

When it comes to the budgetary requirements of government drug information and control services competing against other more glamorous departments of government, the record of appropriations does not favour drug surveillance. On the other hand drug companies can recover in their pricing structure whatever their promotional costs happen to be. Again the contest is uneven and industry wins even against governmental control.

In 1970 the Canadian Government, in a worthy attempt to inform doctors directly about new drugs and about the comparative prices of drugs bearing different advertised trade names, started a monthly journal distributed by mail to each licensed physician in Canada. This was an excellently edited small journal, providing objective information to the physician about drugs, and listing groupings about drugs for comparison in an easily followed table. As a result Canadian doctors had an easy source of reference to guide them in prescribing similar drugs which gave comparative costs. No compulsion was involved and the final choice of the particular brand was left to individual prescribers – a move in the right direction and an attempt at a counter-balance to the promotion of particular brands by the manufacturers of high-cost drugs.

But what happened? Just as this periodical was gaining acceptance among doctors – and incidentally just when the battle of Septra was being fought – the issue of the Canadian Government's Bulletin of October 1973 carried the following note:

> Because of rising costs, it has been necessary to print every second month (formerly every month)... We regret this interruption of service...
>
> The analytical results and drug prices of the Drug Quality Assessment Programme will no longer appear in each issue of Rx Bulletin...

No level of government, no independent journal without advertising, can muster the muscle that industry can and does flex. It is an absurdly one-sided battle.

In the long run every drug is subject to its curve of market acceptance. Every drug sales-curve reaches a peak, remains there for a variable period of time, and then sales begin to fall. Every promoter is aware of this certainty of market performance of anything that is offered for sale. In the long run Septra too will follow this course. But its sales peak is not likely to be depressed in volume or shortened in time by anything that can be accomplished by sober impartial statements in professionally sponsored informational letters, nor by informational material from government sources. These are drowned out by the industrial blare.

There is no comparison between the market clout that can be exerted by the promotional drive of a multinational drug company and the weak forces in opposition. Neither the *Medical Letter* nor the Drug Committee of the Province of Manitoba will have their quiet message heard, surrounded as they are by the continuing blasts of the industrial propaganda.

In the drug industry Burroughs Wellcome may be one of the last of the Mohicans. A scientifically orientated business philosophy was finally overtaken by market-dominated control. This is the only explanation for the major shift in the image of the firm, represented by the aggressive saturation advertising coming from this heretofore low-keyed drug firm. There is little doubt that the promoters in the firm will consolidate and perpetuate their dominance. There is equally no doubt that the profits of the firm, resulting from the change in direction, will show a spurt. It is interesting that this dramatic change occurred in this firm, where the profits are not distributed to shareholders but are directed to a research institute. Profit maximization, in the sense that owners will gain, is not the aim of this firm.

Standards and measures of success by the bureaucracy of firms are undergoing change. For many firms, and the larger are in the forefront, shareholders are no longer important, let alone dominant. The goals that motivate the industrial bureaucracy are 'success' in terms of productivity, sales and, in particular, 'growth'. 'Profits' in the usual meaning of that word are directed into funds for research, development and growth, not into the pockets of shareholders. And, because of risks that may be enormous, a large flow of profits is diverted into reserves for future losses. In this way stability as well as growth is achieved. Shareholders, wherever they exist, are kept quiet by minimal interest payments on their investment, plus the lure of capital gain.

Reserves of money in the vaults of Zürich give a sophisticated investment branch of a company opportunities for further profits out of the capital market. Thus the steady gain in the capital value of the shares on the exchanges, plus the security they are given from an assurance that their money is being stored for them in a safe depository, keeps shareholders happy and in warm anticipation of stock-market gains. Those rising reserves, rather than rising dividends, maintain a market profitability for shares. It is another instance of the importance of aggressive marketing.

In earlier days the drug industry's advertising conformed to the self-imposed restrictions dictated by the pharmacists, who were the leaders in the industry, and according to standards accepted by the medical and pharmaceutical professions. In this way the meaning and concept of the ethical drug firm grew. Its marketing was subdued and its advertising budget minuscule compared with today.

The next stage in the commercial evolution of the drug industry coincides with the rapid growth and development of modern marketing within the whole of the industry. It became clearly apparent in the annual statement that the financial success of the firm was dependent more upon sophisticated aggressive marketing than any other single factor. The control of the policy of the firm passed from owners to a group of professionally trained business administrators. Technostructure became dominated by marketing specialists. Industry generally became market orientated and the marketer rose to top positions in the company hierarchy. The more aggressive he was the better. The high-priced help in the corporate hierarchy are those who can show a rising record of growth in sales in their previous activities. This of course is not surprising. It is in line with goals of our western society. There is no other way the private enterprise system can operate in order to achieve the aim of the two-car family. Our rising standard of living, our accessibility to the new and the better, the promise of rising expectations in the developing world, all of these are largely dependent on the operation of this marketing system.

Within drug-manufacturing firms trouble on an important level occurred. It was the struggle between, on the one hand, the scientifically orientated individuals, subject to the ethics of the scientist, and, on the other, the marketer, directed towards profit and growth. The scientist derives from a university environment and the discipline of science. He regards with some suspicion the so-called mission-orientated research. The scientist out of the university cocoon has been trained to do his 'own thing', to act upon his own hunches and to pursue a trail that may lead to no 'useful' product in the profit sense – but that may uncover and extend the field of human knowledge. There is a profound and important difference between the profit-motivated, mission-orientated research, essential to the industry, and the scientific goal to extend knowledge.

There is evidence that this basic struggle still exists in some of the dominant firms in the drug industry. Even aggressive marketing firms like Hoffman La Roche, and now Burroughs Wellcome, carry out in special laboratories highly important basic scientific research of the best kind. Burroughs Wellcome, through its Wellcome Institute, has an honourable record of research in many areas important to the field of pharmacology and preventive disease. More recently Hoffman La Roche has entered the area of cancer research in an especially built laboratory in the United States. It has discovered important advances in new diagnostic tests for cancer and thyroid diseases – and treatment for a rare condition, systemic candidiasis, that is frequently fatal. Roche estimates these advances will have cost five to six million pounds to produce and will generate at best only 115 thousand pounds a year – certainly not enough to make this part of their research attractive commercially.

This evidence of ambivalence, this digression from conventional commercial wisdom, that says that a buck is a buck is a buck, must represent conflicting ideologies on the second level of the company's decision-making. The primary level is and must be financial gain, and so Roche will adhere tightly to aggressive marketing and the highest possible profitability, and to two of its best money makers – the mood-altering twins Librium and Valium. Serious doubts can be raised about the effects on public health of this class of drug and certainly on the wisdom and even morality of aggressive marketing in this area. They are drugs prominent in any list of suicides, inadvertent over-dosage and the still incompletely researched area of 'falling asleep at the wheel', but they pay for the money-losing research on candidiasis and for the basic research on cancer. This kind of Robin Hood philosophy is probably the best that can be expected under the current system of research, production and distribution of drugs. Nevertheless the relentless extension of this system is frightening.

Are we to face the last decade before Orwell's 1984 with an increasingly drugged society? Is the price of research in cancer to be more and more suicides and deaths at the wheel by wider use of tranquillizers and other money spinners of that dubious kind? And, finally, is the profession of medicine to be included lock, stock and barrel, without a protest, without a wail, without a cry, in the relentlessly encompassing structure of the drug industry? Surely it is not beyond the wit of man to devise some other system for the procurement of needed drugs for society. The answer must lie in complete separation of research from commerce in the drug industry.

Part 2

Controls and the Professionals

8 Who is Minding the Flock?

The Hippocratic Oath was the first expression of the continuing duty of the doctor to his patient. It is a duty that still exists today. It is the creed by which the profession of medicine lays its claim to greatness.

The Hippocratic Oath
I will look upon him who shall have taught me this Art even as one of my parents.

I will share my substance with him and I will supply his necessities, if he be in need.

I will regard his offspring even as my own brethren and I will teach them this Art, if they would learn it without fee or covenant.

I will impart this Art by precept, by lecture and by every mode of teaching, not only to my own sons but the sons of him who has taught me and to disciples bound by covenant and oath, according to the Law of Medicine.

The regimen I adopt shall be for the benefit of my patients according to my ability and judgement, and not for their hurt or any wrong. I shall give no deadly drug to any, though it be asked of me, nor will I counsel such and especially I will not aid a woman to procure an abortion. Whatsoever house I enter, there will I go for the benefit of the sick, refraining from all wrong doing or corruption and especially from any act of seduction, of male or female, of bond or free.

Whatsoever things I see or hear concerning the life of men in my attendance on the sick or even apart therefrom, which ought not to be noised abroad, I will keep silence thereon, counting such things to be as sacred secrets.

The difference between a profession, a craft or a trade can be easily blurred and may not be clearly understood even by professionals themselves. Craftsmen or tradesmen are instructed to perform certain specific acts and are subject to the rules of their employer as to how the job must be done. A professional is consulted with a view to achieving a certain goal, but is not instructed by his client on how this goal is to be achieved. Thus a patient consults a doctor with the aim of restoring health. It is the responsibility of the doctor – and his alone – to determine how. It follows then that it is the doctor's responsibility to decide alone (or with other professional help of his choice) what is the proper medication to be used in the patient's interest. Third-party interference in this professional decision-making process has no place in the transaction. That the third party has, as its legitimate motive, the element of profit-making does not make its advice any more acceptable.

There exist certain irreducible conflicts between ideologies in our society. It is imperative that there must be a continuing and clear distinction between groups that have as their goal the legitimate maximization of profit and those who do not. It is categorically wrong for a doctor to determine his decisions on the basis of practices that enhance financial gain. It is equally categorically right for any industry in our society to seek legitimate financial gain.

As long as a doctor is granted legal right by statute to wield a scalpel on his fellow man, it is absolutely wrong for that scalpel to be used, motivated by profit. No gallbladder, no appendix, no uterus would be safe in its anatomical home were it to be otherwise. On the other hand for profit reasons it is legitimate and acceptable for an industrial firm to place on the market a product that may prove to have serious adverse effects, if wrongly used. Even if rightly used, such a product may be put on the market without complete knowledge of its ultimate effects. This can be done legitimately and for profitable purposes.

This difference in motivation between the medical profession and the drug industry must always exist. It ought to create a legitimate adversary posture between the two. In the legal system the adversary basis in court actions has had to be arbitrarily created between members of the same profession. Lawyers, in the interest of justice for the client, act as adversaries. In the practice of medicine this adversary concept between doctor and drug industry is naturally there. It exists by reason of honest, legitimate, but diametrically opposed, goals. For this reason the medical profession and the drug industry must remain at a decent arm's length relationship.

It is significant that from the earliest history of the medical profession doctors tried to control the prescription and sale and consumption of medications. This has always been a critical function for the doctor. Not only is it his duty to prescribe drugs with due regard for quality and toxicity, but it is his professional responsibility, advised and supervised by his professional associations, to prevent people from swallowing nocuous things sold by irregular practitioners.

This safeguarding of the public by the profession is a duty not sufficiently recognized by the general public or by some members of the profession. In England the exercising of this responsibility and the occasional destruction of the stock of the apothecary (the manufacturer of drugs in early times) and his incarceration in prison led to a state of conflict between doctors and apothecaries that was not resolved for three hundred years. The important element in the doctor–patient relationship was the strict obligation for the individual doctor to survey the drug market actively in order to make certain that no harmful or inferior ingredients would be compounded in the prescription that was dispensed by the apothecary.

What has happened since is a mix of several factors. Firstly, with the disappearance of manufacturing by the apothecary and his conversion into general practitioner, the manufacture of drugs became transferred to chemists, as licensed pharmaceutical chemists, and later to firms who in turn sold their products to pharmacists.

The drug-manufacturing industry thus began partly as a result of shifts within the area of professional responsibility and partly – as with all business endeavours – because it became profitable to manufacture drugs outside the strict professional area of the drugstore or the pharmacy.

With the transfer to the factory, there was no parallel move by doctors in their surveillance over the factory, as there had been supervision over the apothecary. No medical professional organization had the statutory right to enter the factory and destroy its products and jail the manufacturers, as it once had over the manufacturing apothecary.

A further important factor was the enormous development of new drugs, resulting from the birth of scientific synthetic chemistry, whereas in previous years it was mostly so-called botanicals – extracts and brews of various herbs, spices, roots, and so on – that dominated the field (with occasional competition from weird concoctions of animal matter, rotting flesh, both human and animal, animal horns, etcetera). Minerals such as mercury, arsenic, antimony and so one were used only to a small extent.

With this development, chemicals with enormous potential and capacity for creating physiological change – hopefully for the better – began to be elaborated. The chemical industry in Germany was the pioneer in this field and at the turn of this century drugs of proven value and enormous potency, manufactured by the German chemical industry, began to dominate the field. The era of 'scientific medicine' began.

In the twentieth century a notable historical fact – the displacement of the medical profession from its central position of control over medication – was a revolutionary event that took place, ignored by the medical profession itself and unnoticed by the public. It has had the most profound effect on the notion of professionalism as it prevailed within the medical profession. It has radically altered the image of the doctor. It has seriously altered the original concept of doctor–patient relationship. And, finally, it started the chain of events that has resulted in the domination of the profession of medicine by the modern drug industry and created the industrial-medical complex.

There is good reason to believe that this failure of the medical profession to continue its critical supervision over the drug situation and over the proliferation of innumerable products produced by the drug industry is leading to a health-system failure.

Drug Safety and Time-lag

Safety is involved in every drug that is consumed. It is perhaps most important in so-called over-the-counter drugs, which do not require the intervention of a physician to write a prescription. This is a profitable area for the drug manufacturer. In 1969 about two and a half billion dollars were spent in the United States alone on the more than one hundred thousand over-the-counter drugs available. The separation between ethical drug manufacturers, who made and promoted prescription drugs only, and the non-ethical companies that made drugs for unrestricted over-the-counter sale has become blurred. Many companies now do both, if not directly, then through wholly owned subsidiaries.

Furthermore, the separation between drugs that can be sold only with a doctor's prescription and the ones that can be freely purchased at any chemist shop has also become indistinct. As an example, thalidomide could be purchased over-the-counter without prescription in Germany, Spain and in other European and African countries. There still may be shops that have stocks of thalidomide available for sale without prescription, because it was sold under more than thirty different patent names. For many attendants in chemist shops and for most customers the name on the label in no way suggests the drug thalidomide.

In 1972 an English woman holidaying in Spain asked for a remedy for her cold in a local drugstore. She received a medication containing chloramphenicol, an antibiotic limited in its usefulness for rare and specific kinds of bowel infections, including typhoid fever. She received this from the chemist legally without prescription. This drug has a known considerable risk to the blood-forming system and in most countries is not procurable without a prescription. Numerous deaths have been reported, directly attributable to chloramphenicol. In spite of this professionally recognized hazard the lady was sold this remedy by an attendant in a chemist shop in Spain, without requiring a doctor's prescription. She died from the effects of the drug.

Confusion in regulations affecting the sale of drugs between one country and another could be corrected by international agreement. International agreements have been developed in controlling the sale of hard drugs, morphine, cocaine, heroin, and others. It is difficult to understand why similar agreements are not in effect regulating the unrestricted sale of other hazardous drugs such as chloramphenicol.

In many instances until a drug has been conclusively proven to be dangerous it continues to be sold to the public. There is a vast difference between proving a drug dangerous for sale and proving one safe for sale. In the few countries where health authorities prohibit the sale of drugs until they are proven safe, a prolonged and very expensive procedure in order to prove safety must be undertaken by the company holding the patent and seeking the permit for sale. It was this that kept the United States free from the sale of thalidomide. The public health authorities in the United States blocked its release for prescription use until it could be proven definitely safe.

However, to prove safety involves long delays, costly to the drug company, and risks the unhappy possibility that some other drug company will have discovered a new product, claimed to be even better, for the same disease. Spokesmen for drug companies have warned of what they consider to be real disadvantages to the public, resulting from delays necessary to assure safety prior to release.

Professor Milton Friedman, the American economist and champion of free enterprise, dealt with the problem of delay in the distribution of new drugs by placing a money value on the harm that the delay may create. As an example, he stated that, if the introduction of drugs now known to cure tuberculosis had been delayed by two years, according to his calculation, there would have resulted forty-five thousand additional deaths and ninety thousand extra cases of the disease. Furthermore, he stated that the 1962 United States laws requiring drugs to be both safe and effective have cost consumers two hundred to five hundred million dollars a year. No substantial medical evidence was given by the economist for these fantastically large figures.

It is nevertheless interesting to note the vigour with which the drug industry proclaims its case for earlier release of drugs before proof of safety. Where regulations require that the new drug be free from danger, the evidence of danger arrives slowly, often too slowly, and perhaps at a great price in illness and death.

The effect of this attitude creates the situation where the ill must act as guinea pigs to determine whether a drug is dangerous or not. Here the factor of time-lag in communication operates. Time-lag means that hundreds of cases of failure of limb development had to occur before sufficient evidence could be accumulated in order to stop the use of thalidomide. Time-lag meant that many thousands of cases of serious damage to human kidneys occurred, because a frequently used, apparently safe drug, aspirin, was combined with phenacetin. This combination developed enormous sales and profits – and also destroyed thousands of human kidneys. The danger of this combination could have been established without this sacrifice.

Many years may lapse before it is discovered that a drug is dangerous. And during these years many are endangered, made seriously ill or destroyed. It is similar to allowing a strange animal loose among the public and removing it only after it has seriously injured or destroyed. Surely it is preferable to cage the animal until proof of its safety is assured.

With the introduction of every new drug a large amount of information is produced, resulting from accurate testing procedures from within the chemical industry and from animal experiments. Prior to general release of any new medication for prescribing by doctors or for sale over-the-counter, there comes a time when human experiments – a less potentially offensive title is human trial – must be initiated. This is a highly sensitive area.

Human trials are very carefully supervised by trained clinical observers. At first, preliminary tests on volunteers are done, in order to make certain that there are no immediately recognizable harmful effects to any of the human organ systems (blood, heart, liver, kidney and so on). These are usually conducted in a teaching hospital, which is closely associated with a recognized university or medical school. These and subsequent extensions of this human trial are nearly always financed by a grant from the firm developing the particular drug, or by an institute supported entirely or in part by grants from the larger drug-manufacturing firms.

At a later stage in this human experimental process the controlled clinical trial is instituted. The purpose of these formal clinical trials is to separate the few discoveries that will prove to be true advances in treatment from unverified impressions. It is an attempt to determine, in a scientific way, the truth of the safety and effectiveness of a new drug.

Professor Lasagna puts it this way:

Let me try to recapitulate briefly why controlled trials are important. Because few diseases run a course which is precisely predictable; because patients, doctors, and details of medical care differ greatly from place to place, and from one time to another; and because most patients and most physicians are biased towards expecting therapeutic benefit. A properly designed trial is, therefore, an attempt to safeguard the investigator from unwarranted conclusions.

The double-blind trial is one form of the controlled clinical trial. It is especially designed in order that results from the use of the drug should not be biased by the doctors' enthusiasm (or scepticism), nor by the patients' too willing acceptance (or rejection) of anything new; nor by the patients' admiration of the doctor, which may result in a placebo effect. (The placebo effect is a phenomenon that has achieved successful results through many totally inactive drugs, has made millions for drug companies, and has assured a successful practice for those doctors astute enough to make intelligent use of placebo effect in their practice. More will be said about it later.)

The double-blind test demands the use of a dummy product that is totally inert, but that cannot be distinguished in appearance or in taste from the real active drug being tested. It also involves the use of a currently existing drug for the condition in question, and which is also produced for the purposes of the test in a form indistinguishable from the new drug. It is important that the individuals on whom the test is being conducted have, confirmed, the specific disease for which the drug is being tried. A number of patients with – say, high blood pressure – is divided in a random way into three groups. This can be done in a number of ways, the simplest being to number the patients and then to stick red, white or blue pins at random into each number. The red pins get the new drug, the white pins get the dummy and the blue get the existing drug. An absolutely essential part of the trial is that no one, not the doctor, nor the nurse, nor the patient, knows whether they are handling or taking the trial drug.

When the results are collected at a predetermined time, the code is broken. The secret master file that records which patients received the two drugs and which the dummy is revealed. The results are then tabulated in a way that permits unbiased comparison between the effects of the trial drug, the existing drug and the dummy. These results are then subject to rigorous mathematical analysis, according to some generally acceptable method.

The results of the double-blind study may confirm previous assumptions concerning the value of the new drug, or they may completely dash the hopes of the innovators. Some drugs pass the double-blind test, many do not. The new drug must be significantly better than the existing one and better, of course, than the dummy (with its placebo effect). A mere 50 per cent cure rate for the new drug when compared with the old one is not good enough. One can achieve the same degree of success by continuing to use the old drug with either a known risk or no risk of adverse reaction. The new drug should be at least 75 per cent effective and be free from serious toxic or side reactions, before it can justifiably be approved and released for widespread use.

A great many drugs now prescribed freely and profitably have never been subjected to this critical testing. Huge profits can be realized by such drugs, before information becomes available that the new drug represents no real improvement over the drug that it is supposed to replace. It is time-lag that creates sufficient opportunity for many drugs to become financially enormously successful and yet represent no real advance in treatment.

Since the thalidomide disaster, care is taken to determine whether new drugs pass through the placental barrier. Certain drugs taken during pregnancy can be carried by the maternal blood stream into the placenta, the organ that nourishes the developing baby. While in the placenta some drugs may enter into the circulation of the baby by passing the placental barrier, others do not. Obviously it becomes important to know if the proposed drug can pass the placental barrier. If it does, then tests on animals are of paramount importance to determine the effect of the drug on the development of the foetus. If this had been done with thalidomide before it was introduced, the tragedies that thalidomide created might have been avoided.

Unfortunately even this amount of careful experimentation does not give absolute assurance that no teratogenic effect, no distortion of development for the growing baby, will occur. There is a small, unpredictable group of chemical agents that produce no recognizable distortion in the foetus of the experimental animal, but may produce deformities in the human foetus or, like DES (see p. 71), produce its harmful effect one generation removed. It is for this reason that most cautious obstetricians and practitioners forbid any drug in the early stages of pregnancy. Here, a curtailment rather than an increase in the use of drugs may represent the real advance in treatment.

The final proof of drug efficacy and safety may not occur until long after the drug is released for general use to the public. This final stage of *caveat emptor*, 'let the buyer beware', type of mass human experiment comes only after all the preliminary testing has been completed and the drug finally approved by governmental regulatory bodies.

Unfortunately it is an uninformed buyer who must be aware. He has no information, no knowledge, and no appreciation of the risks. He must rely on advertised information alone, with non-prescription over-the-counter drugs. With a prescription, he relies on the professional judgement and conscientious concern of his doctor. In this case the buyer transfers his risk to the professional integrity and knowledge of his own particular physician. How well the doctor discharges this responsibility, or is competent or capable enough to do so, is a variable.

There are hidden factors that enter into every doctor–patient relationship. Circumstances make it very difficult for the great majority of doctors to exercise the required caution, upon which the patient relies, in every written prescription. We have seen that whenever he writes a prescription the doctor is an important part of a system that is geared towards sales, as well as a free professional, exercising scientific and objective judgement. This is not to say that despite the pressures of advertising a doctor is always unaware of the risks involved in the drug he is prescribing. There are hazards in almost all of them. There must be a trade-off between the known risks and the hope for results.

Fortunately, most illnesses or symptoms do not fall within the category of the serious or seriously disturbing, and by far the great majority of illness is self-limiting. They simply disappear by adaptive processes in the human body without any treatment. It is in this very large area of the transient and the trivial that the major disasters may occur. Thalidomide was widely used to relieve anxiety that may certainly have been anything but trivial to the suffering, but was nearly always transient, and would have responded, in a high proportion of cases, to treatment either without drugs or to harmless placebo-type drugs.

With any new drug, even when most of the risks involved are known, or knowable, there is always an undiscovered element of risk not yet known to anyone. Until the drug has been in wide use for a number of years, adverse effects may occur, but remain unknown.

This is due to time-lag in the recording and collection of information about the adverse reactions of drugs. Generally speaking, unless a drug has a very high incidence of unexpected adverse effects (hardly likely if the drug has been tested prior to its release) sporadic adverse effects will pass as unremarkable or attributable to the disease rather than to the drug. Many studies have revealed this time-lag in the collection of information regarding adverse effects.

The thalidomide episode illustrates the time-lag problem. An unusual deformity at birth (phocomelia, or stunting of the limbs) used to be extremely rare. However, it began to be observed with increasing frequency from 1959 onwards, and within three years an increase in the occurrence was noted thus:

	1949 to 1958	*1959 to 1961*
Bonn	0	71
Munich	3	61
Liverpool	0	33

When the increased occurrence of these gross deformities became apparent and, more important, was reported, only then were further studies done and conclusive evidence implicating thalidomide began to be gathered. In questioning forty-six mothers who had deformed babies, it was discovered that forty-one had taken thalidomide in early pregnancy, while similar questioning of 300 mothers who were delivered of normal babies showed that not one had taken thalidomide. Subsequently, experiments on animals were performed that indicated that limb abnormalities of the foetus were almost a certainty, if the mothers were given the drug at an early stage in pregnancy.

In 1964 it was reported that certain coated tablets of potassium (used as a dietary supplement when drugs that increase the flow of urine are administered) caused in some people a narrowing or stricture of the bowel. This was only discovered by looking back into the case records. A sudden unexplained increase in the number of cases of stricture of the bowel were then discovered. In a particular hospital, where this increased occurrence was noted, there were no cases of this particular type of bowel stricture on record prior to 1963, while during the following fifteen months eleven cases were recorded.

In Japan a drug called clioquinol (Entero-vioform) was commonly used and was usually obtained in drug stores without a prescription for common diarrhoea. Thousands of cases of adverse reactions affecting the nerves of the eyes occurred, resulting in some cases of permanently impaired vision. Only then was it discovered that the cause was the frequently used and easily obtainable medication for simple diarrhoea.

In England and in Wales an unexplained rapid increase in sudden deaths in asthmatics has been linked with the use of a particular formulation of aerosol for administering drugs into the lungs of asthmatics. It took three years to link the relationship of these sudden unexpected deaths to the use of this particular agent.

It also took several years to assemble the knowledge that eating soft cheeses, while under treatment by certain drugs for depression, could lead to episodes of high blood pressure that might in some cases result in heart failure or stroke.

In these examples, and in many more, it was only when doctors saw something suspicious or very unusual, following the administration of a certain drug, that curiosity was aroused. Under existing conditions of practice, with over-worked practitioners, the climate for such inquisitiveness rarely exists. Even when the events do occur, they have to occur with such frequency that a 'feeling of surprise' is generated in a sufficient number of practitioners so that they be induced to communicate with each other in some way. Only then can a formal study be undertaken.

It is not surprising, therefore, that several years may elapse before adverse effects of drugs become recognizable, and proper steps can be taken to eliminate or reduce the danger.

In order to help shorten the time-lag in the discovery of these adverse effects the World Health Organization (WHO) set up a drug monitoring organization in Geneva in 1966. This agency, however, must still depend upon observations by individual practitioners, and upon rapid reporting. Regrettably, progress is bound to be slow. It is doubtful that many individual practitioners are even aware of the existence of this international agency, let alone able to recognize adverse side effects each time they occur. Nor can one blame practitioners. It becomes extraordinarily difficult, if not impossible, to distinguish between an adverse reaction to a drug and the effects of the disease itself. Common symptoms, like vomiting or diarrhoea, may be as much a part of the disease as they may be of the medication. It is when a strange symptom, ordinarily not anticipated, supervenes with regularity in this disease, whenever a particular drug is used, that the coincidence of drug and reaction dawns on the observer. This is a slow process. It does not seem likely that this time-lag factor can be appreciably reduced. The old adage, 'stick with the devil (or drug) you know rather than a new one' is still sound advice for the great majority of diseases, and applies to most new drugs on the market.

The time-lag factor is of such duration that by the time a new drug is proven to cause serious adverse side effects, it will have already justified itself financially to the manufacturer. Although certainly not purposely created by the drug firm, time-lag is an important element reducing the financial risk of introducing new drugs. There seems little doubt that if time-lag could somehow be substantially reduced in duration, fewer and safer new drugs would be the result.

There is a profound difference in emphasis affecting the introduction of new drugs between British and American regulations (with Canadian regulations somewhere in between). This was emphasized by the sale of thalidomide. In Britain the distribution of thalidomide was allowed under the regulations; in the United States it was not. The Canadian authorities also permitted distribution, but, under their regulations, could have forbidden it.

In Britain the Committee on Safety of Drugs had been established to ensure, as far as possible, the safety of drugs for illnesses for which they were intended to be used. Its function differed fundamentally from the Food and Drug Administration (United States), which requires that the pharmaceutical company prove not only safety but also effectiveness. That is: that the drug will not poison in the recommended doses and that, in addition, it will be proven to the satisfaction of authorities that it works.

This double-barrelled restraint to the introduction of new drugs in the United States prevented the distribution of thalidomide there (with the exception of the several millions of tablets distributed free to a number of American doctors solely for human trial).

In the United Kingdom in 1968 the watch-dog committee was renamed the Committee on Safety of Medicines, and its regulations were changed to bring it in line with United States regulations: that is that effectiveness, in addition to safety, must be proven by the manufacturer before release of the new drug for general distribution.

However, in spite of the move towards tighter restriction in the United Kingdom – in conformity with United States regulations – many more new drugs are available in the United Kingdom than in the United States. Between 1962 and 1971 nearly four times as many new drugs became available in the United Kingdom as in the United States. Curiously – or perhaps not so curiously – this is the period when thousands of sudden deaths occurred in England and Wales, resulting from the use of an aerosol spray in the treatment of asthma, while relatively few occurred in the United States where the same formulation was not used.

It may be argued that, because of leniency in defining both safety and effectiveness by United Kingdom authorities, there are available to the British public four times as many choices affecting the treatment of their illness than in the United States. There appear to be advances in medical treatment available in the United Kingdom that are not available in the United States. And indeed many drugs are fairly commonly used by doctors in the United Kingdom – apparently to their satisfaction – that are denied to American patients with the same conditions.

The difference between the two national regulatory bodies lies not in the basic regulations, but in the climate of judgement in enforcing these regulations. The difference lies between an attitude of permissiveness in the United Kingdom and relative repression in the United States.

One cannot fault the average individual for being confused about these regulations. He is of course concerned, because after all he is the potential victim or the possible gainer. He must rely on his doctor to make the choice of medication for him. He does this believing the doctor has complete freedom of choice, exercised in the light of complete knowledge of the subject.

Sadly, this is not so. Especially with new drugs. Were it so, the thalidomide tragedy and the asthma aerosol catastrophe would not have occurred in the United Kingdom. The simple fact is that the doctor has had no personal experience and no knowledge of a newly introduced drug, except what is supplied to him by the drug manufacturer, plus what little may be available in the medical literature on the early trials of a drug too new to have shown any adverse effects. In Britain greater reliance is placed by the Committee on Safety of Medicines upon professional freedom, to enable the clinician a wide latitude of judgement regarding new drugs. In the United States on the other hand the Food and Drug authorities are curtailing professional freedom to a degree by a more restrictive approach to new drugs.

Who is right? Well, really no one. On the one hand a more relaxed attitude towards allowing new drugs on the distribution list – as is the case in the United Kingdom – may result in an advance in the treatment of some conditions, and lives may be saved – as Milton Friedman suggests. On the other hand the price is the risk of the too early release of some drugs. In effect the public is used in a guinea-pig manner and catastrophes may occur, and a drug like thalidomide will have caused its havoc before its adverse effects become recognized and appropriate action is taken.

It is not possible to be dogmatic. Perhaps the safest approach with new drugs is to rely on hard-nosed evidence, such as the mortality tables reflecting the state of movement in one direction or another with respect to specific diseases. If earlier treatment with new drugs is what it is cracked up to be, and worth the risk, then over the years the country adopting this permissive attitude ought to show some improvement in the statistical tables respecting that disease. On the other hand a country with a more cautious attitude and with repressive restraints affecting the entry of new drugs would fail to show any improvement in statistical records.

No such help is available. The United Kingdom with the more permissive attitude does not show clear-cut statistical evidence of improvement in its mortality tables. The United States with its more repressive controls on new drugs and consequently with fewer new drugs does not show any worse statistical record of mortality regarding specific diseases compared with the United Kingdom.

For whatever it is worth, the past years have shown two areas of undoubted difference in two diseases between the United Kingdom and the United States – many thousands more cripples from thalidomide, many thousands more sudden deaths from the use of aerosols in asthma, both in the United Kingdom. Curiously, the medical journals have adopted a low profile in their editorial and other comments in this troublesome area and have given little guidance either to the authorities or to doctors. My favourite journal is the *Lancet*. Yet in its issue of 23 March 1974 it philosophizes in its editorial pages under the heading 'Regulating the Introduction of New Drugs' and concludes with this paragraph:

Thus tight and inflexible regulations governing not only the safety but also the efficacy of new drugs may tend to promote therapeutic insularity or even isolationism ... The ideal system of drug control lies between the limits of permissiveness and repression, and it is to be hoped that the relatively relaxed atmosphere which was fostered by the Committee on Safety of Drugs (U.K.) will be preserved by its successor, the Committee on Safety of Medicine.*

That may well be. But the *Lancet* must keep an eye on its advertising contracts for new drugs. Most drug advertising in journals is directed to clarion calls, repeated issue after issue, announcing new drugs. Four times as many new drugs become available in the United Kingdom as in the United States. For an independent journal even of the high quality of the *Lancet*, survival in its present format is dependent almost entirely on the revenue from a high volume of advertising. It gains no revenue from a membership subsidy as does the official journal of a medical association. To reduce the number of new drugs by a factor of four would seriously imperil the life of the *Lancet*. I share with the editors of the *Lancet* the view that this would be nothing short of calamity. But these factors make me uneasy about the *Lancet*'s championing of a 'relaxed atmosphere' towards the acceptance of new drugs in the United Kingdom.

The central problem remains. Two conflicting interests confront each other. One is the thrust of an aggressive industry, researching, manufacturing and promoting drugs for the primary purpose of industrial growth. The other is the safety of the public. In the unequal confrontation between the opposing aims of industry and public safety, the only intervention that can possibly be exerted on behalf of the public relies finally upon the integrity of the medical profession.

* *Lancet*, 1974, i, 493.

The Plight of the Pharmacist

The position of the licensed pharmacist in the health-care system has become ambiguous and a subject for concern. This is due partly to historical trends and partly to the influence and methods of the modern drug manufacturer.

A little more than one hundred years ago in Great Britain pharmacists were called apothecaries. This represents not only a difference in title but a real difference in function. The apothecaries were forerunners of the general practitioner. At that time various societies, for example, The Royal Society of Medicine or the Royal College of Surgeons, provided the specialists for health care. Except in the teaching hospitals and the free-hospital and out-patient departments, specialist care was available only to the wealthy. The great mass of poor relied upon apothecaries for both medical advice and medication.

A description of the out-patient departments in the large London teaching hospitals in the nineteenth century provides an example of the kind of specialist care available to the poor. The sick poor arrived early in the morning and shuffled into a cold, dimly lit hall of a teaching hospital, where they sat on hard backless benches, prepared to wait hours to see the great man.

The specialists on the staff of these hospitals (appointments highly valued for their prestige, rather than for any particular contribution to medical care that could be made in such surroundings) competed with each other to see who could clear the most patients in the shortest time. When the great consultants entered the consulting rooms, an orderly would stand at the front of the hall where the patients were waiting, and bellow, 'Them with the bronchial stand up.' When these people had struggled to their feet he cried, 'Go to the counter to the left for your medicine.' The next shout by the orderly could be, 'Them with the gastric stomachs stand up and go to the counter on the right.' In this manner the common symptoms were called out in succession, until the majority of the patients were cleared out of the room without ever having seen the great man. There were left remaining on the bench, a motley collection that included the deaf who did not hear the shouts, or those with bizarre symptoms that did not correspond to the usual ones called out, or those who were too ill to stand up. These remaining few were then seen by the consultant.

In between the sick poor, who frequented the free-hospital clinics, and the very rich, who could afford qualified members of specialists' societies, were the great mass of people who were cared for by the apothecaries. While there were also individuals called druggists or chemists, who advised and sold drugs, they were at that time generally uneducated and lacked the qualifications to become apothecary practitioners.

In 1834 the apothecaries became recognized as medical practitioners. Their relative importance as practitioners is indicated by the fact that in the years 1842, 1843 and 1844 licences to practise medicine were granted to seven from the University of Oxford, nine from Cambridge, three hundred and thirty-one from Edinburgh and nine hundred and fifty-three from the Society of Apothecaries. In 1858 the Medical Act of Great Britain formally included apothecaries within the category of medical practitioners, and, soon after, no distinction was apparent between the training and qualifications of the apothecary and those of other medical practitioners.

The effect of this change was to leave the dispensing of drugs exclusively to the profession of pharmacy. Pharmaceutical schools and departments of pharmacy of universities train highly qualified individuals with courses that over the years have become more lengthy and scientific in content. At the present time a degree in pharmacy takes an average of four years' attendance at a university or approved institute. This is almost the same length of time required for a degree to practise medicine.

But in the light of these lengthening, highly sophisticated courses in dispensing, what indeed has happened to the duties required of a qualified pharmacist in today's pharmacy or drugstore? No longer does he exclusively and expertly mix ingredients for a prescription. No longer does he manufacture his own tinctures or make ointments or creams. His task, simply stated, has become counting, measuring, recording and accounting. Almost invariably, now, the prescription states the single name of a preparation, pre-packaged by the manufacturer in the commonly prescribed quantity and dosage. All that is required of the pharmacist is that he check the prescription against a possible error in dosage by the prescriber, take from his shelf the correct package, or count into a container the prescribed number of pills, write or type a label, record the prescription in a book and file the original prescription, now numbered to correspond with the number on the label.

Even when the procedure is rhetorically elaborated, as below, in order to justify a prescription fee (and there is no doubt that a prescription fee for this service is fully justified) is there real need for a full four-year programme of study to perform the following act?

1. THE DISPENSING FUNCTION *

Although requiring much less in the form of manipulative skill than formerly, the actual dispensing function must still be regarded as the keystone of the pharmacist's service role. The dispensing function is usually defined as including the sequence of tasks beginning with the receipt of a prescription order from the physician and culminating with the issue of the packaged medication to the patient. The sequence includes the following:

a) Receiving and Authenticating the Prescription

Although physicians frequently will give the prescription to the pharmacist over the telephone, the majority of prescriptions received in the pharmacy are written orders. In the case of some narcotics, the pharmacist can only accept a written prescription. In a study carried out for the Commission it was found that the relative proportions were 22·8 per cent by telephone and 77·2 per cent written prescriptions. It is the pharmacist's responsibility to assure himself that the prescription will be dispensed for the person named and that it is one he may legally accept for filling. The signature of the physician, or his voice in the case of telephoned prescriptions, must be known to the pharmacist, or he must take any necessary steps to verify same. Many pharmacists now maintain patient medication records and the patient's card will be pulled from the file when a new prescription order is received.

b) Interpreting and Checking

* The above is taken from the chapter entitled 'Dispensing Function', from the Report of the Commission of Pharmaceutical Services of the Canadian Pharmaceutical Association, June 1971.

Care must be taken to insure that the physician's intentions are properly interpreted. This step involves both the deciphering of writing and correct interpretation of the drug(s) ordered. The pharmacist must be on guard with regard to look-alike, sound-alike names (e.g. Preludin is an appetite depressant and Proluton is an oral hormone product; Tensilone is indicated for high blood pressure and Tensilon is a powerful antagonist of curare which, itself, is a very potent muscle relaxant). In the preliminary examination of the prescription the dose prescribed must be carefully checked (having in mind whether the patient is a child or an adult) and any necessary calculations made. In the event of any uncertainty as to the physician's intention or when an error is detected, the pharmacist will contact the physician.

c) Numbering the Prescription and Preparing the Label –
Prescriptions are numbered in sequence as they are dispensed. This number and the date will be entered on the label together with the name of the patient and the name of the physician. In addition to the prescriber's directions for use, the pharmacist will label any other instructions his knowledge of the product indicates (e.g. refrigerated storage, keeping out of direct sunlight, etc.).

2. PREPARATION OF THE MEDICATION
The great majority of prescriptions now require merely the dispensing of a ready-made dosage form, prepared by a manufacturer and stocked in quantity by the pharmacist for dispensing in smaller quantities [emphasis mine]. Sometimes the prescription can be dispensed in the original container, but usually, an appropriate compounding is required, the proper ingredients must be assembled and correct pharmaceutical techniques utilized. In both cases careful identification of the ingredients used is essential to avoid error. Where the matter is within his discretion, the pharmacist will select the brand of a product to be dispensed.

3. RECORDING
The number of the prescription, the price charged, and the pharmacist's initials are placed on the original prescription, together with any notations that may be necessary if the prescription is one which may be refilled. The patient's medication record card will be also completed at this stage. Regulations pertaining to restricted drugs require that certain record forms be entered. Third-party payment forms, income-tax receipts and other paper-work require attention at this stage.

4. DELIVERY TO THE PATIENT

Prior to delivering the prescription to the patient the pharmacist will usually double-check the finished prescription against the prescription order. In the process of transferring the package to the patient the pharmacist should communicate any necessary cautions with regard to storage and use, warnings with regard to interfering foods, in order that the patient will clearly understand how it is to be used. In a study, carried out for the Commission, it was found the great majority of prescriptions were being delivered to the patient (or his agent) in the pharmacy. Only 13·1 per cent were delivered to the patient's home. It may be said of the dispensing function, in general, that it calls for a high degree of professional judgement and that it must be assumed that the pharmacist will aways retain responsibility for the entire process. While it is coming to be recognized that the pharmacist may divest himself of the physical operations involved, there is unanimity of opinion that he cannot divest himself of the responsibility itself and must maintain clear supervision throughout by checking work at various stages.

Four years of university training for this? Surely this is a massive waste of educational resources and student time to prepare a group of intelligent individuals to perform just that essential act. Advances in the drug-manufacturing industry have greatly simplified dispensing of prescriptions. In addition doctors have increasingly accepted industrial urging to prescribe, by patent names, pre-packaged parcels of drugs in the commonly used dosage and quantity. Because of the successful effect of promotion upon the physician who writes the prescription, more than one half of all the prescriptions comprise only about eighty separate entities. Some of the mood-affecting drugs appear so frequently in the succession of prescriptions in the pharmacist's dispensary, they could easily be dispensed by pressing a button.

Were there a cultural content in the professional pharmaceutical courses there might be extenuating circumstances. But, like all technological courses from medicine through to engineering, the cultural content, if there ever was one, has been squeezed out by the relentless advance of technology. With greater specialization in all these areas more and more is taught about less and less. But while other technological areas such as medicine and engineering have been providing trained individuals for expanding fields of technology, the same is not true in the field of pharmacy. The main purpose of the course, the dispensing function, has become narrowed and almost completely absorbed by the manufacturing process. Four years of training are hard to justify, for the diminishing amount of scientific and technological knowledge required for modern dispensing.

This is not a plea to abbreviate the training programme of the pharmaceutical dispenser. But it should be pointed out: in the training and knowledge of the pharmacist a vast potential of real value to our public-health system lies fallow. This potential remains lamentably unused in the simplified performance of modern dispensing. There can be real improvement in the delivery of health care, with the advantage of professional enhancement for the pharmacist. A modification in the course of pharmacy in two important areas of function deserves exploration.

The first affects the sale of over-the-counter drugs. The second deals with the development of professional advisors towards rational prescribing (the prescribing of the right drug to the right patient at the right time and for the lowest cost).

The volume and variety of drugs sold without the requirement of the prescription – the so-called over-the-counter drugs – is huge. These drugs vary in toxicity from products with a possibility of serious over-dosage to products that are inert agents having only placebo effect. Most of these are now manufactured by the larger drug firms, or by subsidiary companies of the larger firms, and are the subject of intensive advertising over the mass media. Most of the advertising has no basis in scientific fact – but, as long as the claim for them in the advertisements can conform to the permissive regulations of governmental regulatory bodies, they are allowed uninhibited promotion and sale. The main objection to them is that they extract large amounts of money from consumers who are in no position to make a rational judgement regarding their value. They continue to sell and may indeed have a very long market life, because the illnesses for which they are usually used have a short natural course. They are dis-eases that are composed of transient discomforts from short self-limited illnesses: the common cold, minor stomach upsets, party hangovers, temporary headaches and muscular aches and pains, and so on. The medicine man sold his snake oil on the same basis.

But these over-the-counter drugs have an important function in the health-care system. They provide an opportunity for a large proportion of those suffering from dis-eases to have early contact with a professional, in this case a qualified pharmacist. Here is a golden opportunity for the exercise of clinical triage during the earliest stage in dis-ease.

'Triage', in its medical sense, is not yet defined as such in the Oxford English Dictionary. It derives from a useful concept in military medicine. When, during a battle, casualties in large numbers arrive at a forward medical station close to the battle area, a medical officer, on the basis of rapid but experienced assessment, divides the casualties into one of three groups. The first group is so seriously wounded that no conceivable treatment has any chance to save life. These are given an injection of morphine to quieten apprehension and ease pain, but nothing more is done. The reason for this apparent callous disregard of life is related to the demands imposed by the battle occasion. Given the scarce availability of medical help at the spot, it would seriously impair the chances of those less seriously injured, if time were taken and the meagre resources consumed in an effort to save a life that is moribund.

The second group is the wounded for whom there exists a reasonable chance to save life or limb. These are also administered pain-relieving medication and early emergency care is given, such as arrest of haemorrhage, etcetera. This group is then quickly sent on to a hospital behind the forward lines where formal treatment can be provided.

The third group in this process of triage includes those with minor injuries that can be dressed or bandaged. The individuals in this group are quickly returned to the fighting area to maintain military strength.

The word 'triage' is now frequently used in the emergency and admitting areas of the larger urban hospitals to divide patients into three groups. One requires immediate resuscitation and admission into hospital; another may be held for observation and tests in the admitting ward before a decision for disposal can be made, and a third group with minor illnesses requires only simple medication without admission to a hospital.

Although it is rarely recognized, the pharmacist acts as a forward triage officer in civilian practice. For many patients he is the first person of contact in their illness. He is convenient, he is a professional, and one does not have to make a prior appointment and wait. Many pharmacists develop valuable clinical experience of real importance in the health-delivery system. On this first contact they make important decisions whether to advise the patient to proceed to hospital immediately, or to make an appointment with their doctor, or to recommend the use of an over-the-counter drug. This is a form of medical triage currently carried out, to the best of their abilities, by pharmacists. In a roundabout and modified way he may be repeating the historic function of the apothecary of a hundred and fifty years ago. It was an important function then – it could become an equally important function now.

There is great potential value in recognizing this asset existing in the person and training of the pharmacist. At a time when medical care is becoming more and more specialized, when primary contact with the physician is difficult, increasingly costly, time consuming and unequally distributed, the occasion has arrived to make better use of the potential skills of a professionally trained person, who spends four years in a university or equivalent area as part of his professional equipment. This skill is now employed in writing labels and dispensing pre-packaged goods out of his dispensary.

With modification in course content, but without making the training programme any longer, the pharmacist could develop into a qualified triage officer at the first line of contact with many patients. Even without this specialized training, in many instances, he today serves this function for the thousands of individuals who ask him what is good for a headache, stomach-ache, cough, sore muscle, and so on – the common complaints of millions who are wheedled, cajoled and badgered by the advertising programmes of the drug firms eager to sell their particular brand of snake-oil. The pharmacist can use his knowledge, his professional integrity and his advice to protect the consumer from commercially motivated blandishment. He could also protect the individual from more drug taking, when it is medical investigation or hospital treatment that is clearly mandatory. In this respectable new function the pharmacist can gain an importance in the health-delivery system without moving from his primary base, the chemist shop or the drugstore, and without incurring further investment in time or capital.

The second goal, but requiring a further expenditure in postgraduate training, may qualify some graduate pharmacist for the area of therapeutic specialist, or advisor to the medical practitioner in initiating or changing drug treatment. It is ludicrous that at the present time this function is performed mainly by relatively untrained company representatives or detail men. One has only to walk through the halls of any teaching hospital today and see the clusters of residents and doctors being 'educated' on therapy by well-meaning, but basically uninformed, company representatives or detail men employed by industry, in order to realize that this is an essential function that requires better handling.

This new status for the pharmacist is already starting in some teaching hospitals, where pharmacists sit on therapeutic committees and give their advice on the selection of a particular drug from a large list that can be used for a specific disease. This can be extended to the point where a pharmaceutically trained therapeutic specialist, having made a special and continuing study of the multiplicity of new drugs on the market, can advise the busy practitioner which particular one out of the many is the appropriate medication. The doctor and the patient could thus have the benefit of a professional with specialized experience in drugs.

One may object that this kind of advice infringes on the function of the doctor. That may be true. It is equally true that this exercise of professional opinion without industrial bias is now more observed in the breach than in the performance. The average doctor performs as a true professional up to the point of writing a prescription. From that point on he has become so programmed by commercial propaganda to sell particular products that intervention by another professional at this stage can only improve the quality of health care.

In time the pharmaceutically trained specialist may also prove to be a focal point in collecting and assessing two streams of information. The first is concerned with the efficacy of new drugs. The second stream of information comes from patients' reactions to drugs, especially new drugs. Drug information centres, staffed by pharmacists and supported by non-industrial subsidy, have already begun to function in some medical educational centres. These centres gather information about drugs, about adverse effects, about toxicity. They also gather information about specific allergic reactions that some people have from certain groups of drugs. This information can be stored in a computer bank and retrieved and made available rapidly, in the same way that somewhere, somehow, a computer screams if you exceed the allowable limits of your credit-card purchases. Such an information bank may prevent over-dosage in the event that the patient (unknown to the prescribing doctor) is already taking the identical drug with another trade name. If, at the moment of prescribing, a rapid information system were available to the doctor, telling him that on the previous day the patient had received a similar sedative or a similar pain killer prescribed by another doctor, much of the harmful repetitive prescribing and unintended over-dosage could be prevented. Unnecessary hospital treatment and tragic risk to life from overuse could be prevented.

Such centres, administered and staffed by specialist pharmacists, could greatly reduce the ever increasing number of iatrogenic diseases (diseases caused by medical treatment). These have been estimated to cause 15 to 20 per cent of hospital usage. Economists may calculate the colossal saving of financial, technical and professional resources that could be achieved, but much more important is the saving of human suffering and even life itself.

One cannot rely either upon industry or government to initiate and effect the change that could redeem a profession and restore it to its deserved position in the medical health system. The change will come only when enough individual pharmacists demand it and initiate the appropriate action by their professional associations. As long as individual pharmacists remain unaware of the plight of their profession; as long as the 'front store', the sale of sandwiches, popcorn, stationery supplies, even pitchforks and shovels is a main concern; as long as creating and satisfying the wants of more and more consumers continues to be their source of prosperity – they will flourish as entrepreneurs. But as professionals they will be destroyed. Only a new awareness by individual pharmacists of the importance of the integrity of their calling to society will redeem the profession of pharmacy.

9 Public Health

Where are We?

The phenomenal growth of the drug industry; the immense increase in new drug, research; the choking of our information-gathering storage and retrieval system by the massive volume of research reports; the dominating position by industry over governments, over professionals and over the ill – with all of these overpowering factors at work, what has been achieved positively for the health of the public? Real gains in public health are complicated and difficult to measure. We are all too easily seduced into accepting the blare of publicity devoted to heart operations and the fanfare introducing the newest series of 'wonder drugs' as evidence of real progress.

There are, however, several criteria that can be used as possible yardsticks of progress in public health resulting from new drugs and new treatments. One is a review of the statistics dealing with life and death. In those countries where such records are accurately collected the evidence can be impressive and may be conclusive.

If a significant decline in deaths from a particular disease coincides with the discovery and application of a new treatment, it can usually – but not always – be accredited to that treatment. The reason for the 'not always' is that some diseases have a way of waxing and waning in their occurrence over a span of time for as yet unknown reasons. For example, the number of cases and, in consequence, the deaths from cancer of the stomach mysteriously declined significantly in some countries. On the other hand the diminution of new cases and reduction in deaths from tuberculosis can confidently be attributed to the factors of early recognition and the development of reliable curative drugs, along with improved preventive measures.

Once we have left this area of hard, uncontestable death-rate as a measure of efficiency of any treatment, we immediately enter a woolly land of opinion and speculation, subject to all kinds of error, not least of which is the understandable human desire to see improvement when none exists.

As an example of just one of these problems affecting accurate scientific assessment of the value of any drug, let us look at the placebo effect. Let us assume that we wish to test the effects of a particular drug upon one thousand individuals with the common cold. The best way to do this is by the method known as a controlled clinical trial, of which 'double-blind testing' is probably the most accurate. So far, whenever this kind of controlled clinical trial has been performed on any of the drugs frequently advocated and universally used for the common cold, the results have shown the same rate of cure for the dummy drug as for the new drug being tested.

The improvement in those taking the dummy drug is called the 'placebo effect'. The placebo effect is even more complicated than it sounds and to a varying degree it is a factor in the response to any treatment, even surgical. The inexplicable and mystifying element about the placebo effect is that it may even favourably alter the physical evidence of the disease. It creates not only relief of pain and discomfort – the subjective evidence of disease as reported by the patient – but it frequently affects, in a beneficial way, measurable things like blood pressure, rate of respiration, sweating, and temperature. These are usually considered to be factors that are not subject to control by the patient himself. These factors comprise the objective evidence of disease. Even such measurements as increase in white-blood-cell count or prolonged sedimentation rate (both being frequently used tests for inflammatory disease) have been brought back to normal as a result of placebo treatment. Complex interactions, as yet only guessed at, occur between the psychological state or psyche of the patient and his physiological state. Placebo effect has been known to influence such physiological functions as the pressure of the blood stream, the movement of bowels, the passage and chemistry of urine and even such intricate factors as the constituents of the blood.

The placebo effect has sometimes been observed in association with the image of the kindly, respected family doctor, whose mere presence makes many people feel better and actually makes some of them physically better. The placebo effect may be predominant in any trial of new drugs and confuses the statistics of the efficiency of many of them, especially when the drug has become emphasized in popular media, the press, radio and television, and in professional journal advertising, as a real breakthrough in treatment – as a new 'wonder drug'.

A part of the favourable results following surgical treatment may be due to placebo effect. One has only to read the list of abandoned abdominal operations that used to have acceptance as preferred treatment and following which many patients felt better. Nor can one say with certainty that some of the surgical procedures performed today do not rely to varying degree for their success on placebo effect. As in the past, so in the future, many of today's accepted treatments (be they by drugs or surgery) will undoubtedly be discontinued, because the effects now claimed will prove to be placebo in nature.

For acceptable scientific proof of effectiveness in treatment the drug or the procedure must predictably and consistently alter the natural course of the disease. It must beneficially alter the physiological state of the patient by changing or by removing the agent causing the disease. Proven drugs – penicillin, sulfonamides, insulin, digitalis, etcetera – belong to a rather small and select group. While the placebo effect may still be operative with each, it is an adjunct to the more scientifically predictable action of the agent itself. All these drugs in specific diseases will give consistent results upon testing in any randomized clinical trial or double-blind testing.

But what of the overall situation? Is there any way that the effect of the increasing number of new drugs, promoted and used since the turn of the century, can be assessed in terms of improvement in public health or in terms of increase in life expectancy? As a cold economic question – has the expenditure of billions, the input of vast physical and human resources and the development of an aggressive drug industry resulted in an output of sufficiently improved health or sufficiently improved life expectancy?

Or has there been an enormous mis-use of scarce human and physical resources in these areas of professional and drug-industry endeavour? Can the state of public health be subject to critical analysis and not merely to wishfully motivated hosannas of triumph?

This is a disturbing question. The answer is not easy. Indeed with the present state of our methods of assessment the answer may not be possible. It must be admitted that we still do not know whether the vast and growing expenditures upon increasing technological advance are creating real gains in public health. Nor on the other hand is it certain they are not. Clearly there is need for humility on both sides. Certainly the champions of the drug industry need to develop a humbler posture in claiming improvements resulting from the activities of the industry.

If there were clear evidence of social gain from the increasing use of drugs, the righteous posture of the industrial-medical complex would be more secure. But what is the hard evidence of gain? Is there positive evidence that the total health picture has improved, to balance the huge costs of the increase in drug research and of increased drug consumption?

The answer to this important question is a mixed one. On the plus side there is, in two areas of treatment, impressive evidence of positive gain in public health. The first is in the treatment of tuberculosis. The second is in the treatment of acute infections by antibiotics. Most of the gain in public health has been in the age groups where these two conditions are prominent (up to about forty-five years of age). The drug treatment of tuberculosis has almost entirely eliminated the disease in those areas in the world where the treatment is applied. Here the sanatoria have emptied. The results with other microbic diseases are also favourable, but not quite so striking, because here the situation is complicated and more difficult to analyse. Virus diseases, as yet not amenable to drug treatment, are gradually replacing the microbic infections that have been eliminated by antibiotic drugs. Furthermore, periodic outbreaks of varieties of microbic infections, resistant to the known antibiotics, have made the picture of infectious disease even less clear. However, in the field of acute infection, an area of gain seems clear, although subject to qualifications.

While some of the reduction in infectious diseases is due to preventive factors, resulting mainly from improved sanitation and nutrition, on balance it is probable that acute infectious diseases and tuberculosis are an outstanding example of significant improvement in public health caused by the research, promotion and wide use of appropriate drugs.

In no other area of medical treatment can it be proved to hardnosed statisticians and epidemiologists (those who deal with disease as it affects populations) that there is a real area of substantial gain in total health that is with certainty due to recent drug discoveries.

Another part of the problem of accurate assessment of improvement in public health is that a scientific definition of 'improvement' is impossible to establish, except in terms of prolongation of life. We can get accurate statements of rising or falling death rates for any disease. But to get accurate numerical accounts of illness or, more difficult still, an accurate or direct account of dis-ease, of feeling unwell, or just plain lousy, is impossible. In this area we must rely on less accurate and on indirect evidence, such as hospital admission rates for various diseases and figures that tell us the number of days off work or the amount paid in compensation for industrial disability, or unemployment due to health reasons.

Immediately, it becomes apparent that such figures are not reliable. Although they may indicate trends in the success or failure rate of drug treatment, these figures get terribly mixed up with social attitudes towards work, holidays, desire for admission to hospital, and the understandable tendency of physicians to accept the statements from their patients that they are too ill to work, even though the doctor may have silent doubts.

There are social styles and attitudes that affect disability. It was firmly believed several generations ago that one worked until one dropped. The work ethic was prominent, and insecurity was perhaps so much greater that to stay off work aroused a certain amount of suspicion that one was lead-swinging or just simply being lazy. Furthermore, idleness was such a nasty word that one tended, in illness, to work long past the moment when one would stop work today. Such changes in attitude can significantly skew figures for disability or for time off work and make these kinds of statistics very much less accurate than the hard statistic of death.

Is There a Powles or a Cochrane in the House?

In the theatre a few generations ago, it was not unusual for the audience to be so moved by the cliff-hangers in the horse-operas that illness would occur among the more susceptible. Whenever this happened a member of the staff would climb the stage and shout, 'Is there a doctor in the house?' In an admittedly far-fetched analogy, we need a new kind of doctor to help the total social audience in the current passing show – a kind of doctor who can deal with diseases as they affect the audience, society, rather than the single individual – a kind of doctor who sees heart attacks, high blood pressure, infections, and even cancer as being related in a variable but increasingly important degree to environmental factors. If premature hardening of arteries finally terminates in a fatal heart attack, is not the actual 'disease' those elements in our social and physical environment that accelerate arterial hardening? If the pace of modern life, if faulty diet, lead to conditions that cause premature death, are they not the real culprits, rather than the intermediate hardening and thickening of arteries?

These are challenging concepts. They run slap-bang against the increasingly brisk pace of modern technological advance in medicine – more drugs, more active-care hospitals, more intensive-care centres. To buck a trend that has such wide acceptance within our culture, that affects the training of doctors and nurses, a giant drug industry, and that is based upon popular consent and government acquiescence, is tough and requires guts. There is today a small phalanx of such doctors, who are not only tough but use, as instruments, sharp facts that are hard to counter.

Dr A. L. Cochrane, Director of the United Kingdom Research Council Epidemiology Unit, and Dr John Powles, Research Fellow, Centre for Social Research, University of Sussex, are two such doctors. These and a few others are making important contributions in this crucial area, by an attempt at reasoned, factually based assessments of health benefits to society compared to costs – human as well as monetary. The questions they pose demand critical review of the factors that for many years we have accepted as 'gains'.

John Powles says: 'One of the more striking paradoxes facing the student of modern medical culture lies in the contrast between the enthusiasm associated with current development, and the reality of decreasing returns to health from rapidly increasing efforts.' *

A. L. Cochrane puts it another way: 'I asked a worker at a crematorium who had a curiously contented look on his face, what he found so satisfying about his work; he replied that what fascinated him was the way in which so much went in and so little came out. He probably got his kicks from a visual demonstration of the gap between input and output.'†

What indeed is the record of improvement in public health, compared to vast expenditures by doctors, nurses, technicians and on output for buildings and equipment, and, last – but certainly not least – the rapidly increasing input of drugs into this massive health machine?

There are many figures for the consumption of drugs, all showing the same trend: upwards. Perhaps the most reliable, because it represents a reasonably stable population, come from the United Kingdom, when in the years from 1959 to 1969 there was a growth in the number of prescriptions written, from two hundred and fourteen million to two hundred and sixty-four million, an increase of approximately 25 per cent.

This expenditure, representing the use of scarce resources and sophisticated manpower, ought to be followed by some evidence of improvement in public health. Is there clear statistical evidence of improvement?

The answer to this important question is an unsatisfying 'yes and no'. There are a few positive factors and some negative ones.

* 'On the Limitations of Modern Medicine', *Science, Medicine and Man*, Vol. I, Number I, April 1973, p. 1, Pergamon Press.

† *Effectiveness and Efficiency*, Nuffield Provincial Hospitals Trust 1972, p. 12.

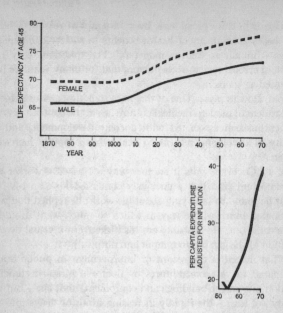

Figure 1: Mortality trends since 1870 (England and Wales) with superimposed expenditure trends constructed from National Health Service (United Kingdom) per capita expenditure since 1950*

Let us consider the figures affecting mortality since 1870 in England and Wales – approximately the past one hundred years.

In two areas there have been unmistakable positive gains: a reduction in infant mortality and a reduction of deaths from acute infectious diseases. Referral to the graph illustrated in figure 1 will reveal several facts.

By far the greatest improvement in the past century has been a marked drop in infant mortality. This is most evident if we examine the steep decline in deaths, especially since 1900.

* From Powles, John, 'On the Limitations of Modern Medicine', *Science, Medicine and Man*, Pergamon Press, 1973, Vol. 1, pp. 1–30. Powles adds the following note with reference to his compilation regarding the above graph.

'Life expectancies from Office of Population Censuses and Surveys,

This period coincides with the period of increased technology in medical care, more and better hospitals, and improved training and standards for midwives with better accessibility to the discoveries in preventative care and treatment of infectious diseases.

But this interval also coincides with important and significant improvement in environmental factors, better nutrition, improved sanitation, better control of the purity of water and milk, and a growing public acceptance of birth-control measures resulting in smaller families.

It is not easy to determine which of these factors is the more important – the improvement in medical technology or the improvement in environmental factors. The increase of medical technology has resulted in better hospital care and the development of antibiotics and immunization. This has coincided with definitely improved life expectancy for children. But the real value of these technical and medical factors, depending on the growth of the drug industry, is challenged by referral to figure 2.

Here there is evident a progressively steady decrease in deaths, under the age of fifteen, from four childhood infections – scarlet fever, diphtheria, whooping cough, measles – in the years from 1850 to 1965.

The introduction of antibiotics and immunization against diphtheria, as indicated by the arrow during the 1940s, seems to have made no significant change in the rate of decline of mortality of these diseases. Ninety per cent of the improvement in death rate had already occurred prior to the introduction of immunization and the use of antibiotics. While not denying the

Registrar General's Statistical Review for England and Wales for the Year 1970, Part II, "Tables Population", H.M.S.O., London, 1972 Table B2.' Infant Mortality rates are from the same source, Part I, 'Tables Medical', Table 3. N.H.S. Expenditure for the United Kingdom by Calendar Years is from *Office of Health Economics*, 'Information Sheet 15', December 1971. Expenditure is standardized using Consumer Price Index from *Central Statistical Office, National Income and Expenditure*, 1971, H.M.S.O., London, 1971, Table 16. As costs within the Health Service increase more rapidly than consumer prices generally, the graph will overstate the true rise in real expenditure – perhaps by 20 to 30 per cent.

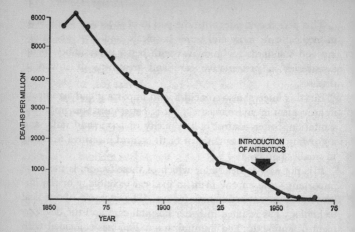

Figure 2: *Deaths of children under fifteen years attributed to scarlet fever, diphtheria, whooping cough and measles. (England and Wales) From Porter†

usefulness of immunization and antibiotics for a share of the improvement in child mortality, it seems obvious that other factors were already creating a favourable effect prior to the introduction of these agents. It is not, as protagonists of the drug industry have claimed, an undivided victory for the industry.

Kwashiorkor is an illustration of a modern disease related to environmental factors. Although the figures for its occurrence vary from time-to-time, it is probably the most common children's disease in the world. It is caused by a deficiency in protein plus reduced calories in the diet of millions of youngsters in many tropical countries where there is a scarcity of animal protein. The modern name for the disease is 'protein-calorie-

* From Powles, John, 'On the Limitations of Modern Medicine', *Science, Medicine and Man*, Pergamon Press, 1973, Vol. I, pp. 1–30.

† Porter, R. R., 'The Contribution of the Biological and Medical Sciences to Human Welfare', *Presidential Addresses of the British Association for Science*, Swansea Meeting, 1971, published by The British Association, 1972, p. 95.

malnutrition', but 'kwashiorkor' is not only more colourful, but more expressive of the basic responsible factor: it means in African dialogue (Ghana) 'second baby came too soon'. This illustrates the social factor in the cause of this disease – absence of birth control. As long as the baby is breast fed, and receives its quota of essential protein and calories, it is a normal, often plump, healthy infant. The crisis in this baby's life occurs when the 'second baby arrives too soon' and replaces the first one at the breast. Baby number one must now compete with older and stronger members of the family for the limited amount of protein food that is available. In this tough feeding competition it nearly always gets pushed aside and so suffers from this kind of protein lack at a stage in its development when proteins are essential for body growth. The malnutrition can be of several degrees of severity, but its chief danger is a severe lack of resistance to ordinary infection and serious complications from minor accidents.

Kwashiorkor thus illustrates all three factors in creating a high death rate in childhood: frequent pregnancy, poor diet and lack of resistance to infection. These are the three grim apocalyptic horsemen of death for children in poorer countries. Here is an illustration of preventable, and in the early stages, curable disease that requires no medication – simply a recognition that the real disease is environmental and the disease process is not really kwashiorkor – the end stage – but starvation, absence of birth control and poor resistance to infection.

Western society's weak grasp of these factors as the real diseases and the heavy reliance upon engineering technology in our medical teaching are also illustrated by this disease. Although kwashiorkor is certainly one of the most common medical diseases affecting the world's children, a standard textbook of Medicine – *Harrison's Principles of Internal Medicine* (McGraw Hill, United States, sixth edition) devotes less than two pages out of its two thousand to a description of the disease. Furthermore, when periodic epidemics of this disease decimate children of the developing countries, well-intentioned people, brainwashed by the drug industry, send, instead of proteins, millions of vitamin pills – as effective for this disease as a spit in the ocean.

Referring again to figure 1, the nearly horizontal line at the top of the graph represents life expectancy when calculated at the age of 45 (the dotted line for females and the solid line for males). These two lines are highly significant. They show very little improvement during the last one hundred years, with the exception that the life expectancy of the female continues to improve slightly over the male. The average period of widowhood has increased from 5·59 years in 1932 to 8·25 years in 1968. In spite of all the glittering advances in technology, with increase in active treatment hospitals, with 'improvement' in the treatment of heart attacks by the establishment of literally thousands of costly, intensive-care cardiac units in many hospitals, with widely advertised new drugs produced by the drug industry – the death rates for middle-aged men are failing to improve and indeed in several countries have become marginally worse.

There is undisputed improvement in life expectancy, providing the calculation is made from the day of birth, as indicated in the lower pair of the nearly parallel lines in figure 1 – (the dotted for the female and the solid for the male). In other words a child born in 1870 had an average life expectancy of 40 years while a child born in 1970 had an average expectancy of about 70 years – a distinct improvement. But if one compares this with life expectancy calculated from the age of 45, there has been no improvement. This apparent contradiction is due to the fact that many more individuals now reach the age of 45 as a result of the improved infant mortality rate; but from the age of 45 on their chances are about the same today as they were a hundred years ago.

How does this compare with the claims of the industry regarding improved new drugs for that formidable array of killing diseases that wipe us out after the age of 45 – the heart, lung and blood vessel diseases and cancer?

Sadly, this graph, based on hard, cold figures of mortality, declares that there has been no significant improvement in the treatment of diseases occurring after the age of 45 – not enough to deflect mortality figures.

A solid, substantial increase that the graph in figure 1 does show, at the extreme right, is an almost vertical line of cost increase for health in the years of 1950 to 1970. In England and Wales for those twenty years, there has been an increase in costs amounting to more than three hundred per cent with increased expenditure on hospitals amounting to almost four hundred per cent. Drug expenditures outside of hospitals increased by almost five hundred per cent.

It is true that much of this expenditure, while having little or no impact on improvement in health, as reflected by an improved mortality rate, has helped many individuals to cope with their illnesses and has made the ill 'feel better'. These are worthwhile goals. But for the record, and for the sake of public understanding of drug-industry claims, these are the sobering facts of life and death. The effect of new drugs in the past quarter century should be considered in the light of this evidence.

As for the second level of figures – the ones having to do with sickness rates – the conclusions are at best vague. Our health, according to these criteria, has actually deteriorated in the past twenty years. Days off work for certified illness per 100 men in Great Britain has increased from 1279 in 1954 to 1632 in 1967 – an increase of 127 per cent. Hardly an improvement, even accepting the unreliability of this indicator of ill health.

Without labouring the point too much, there seems little to substantiate the rosy vista of a world made healthier by drugs, so optimistically illustrated by the public relations men and advertising copywriters of the drug industry. When one also considers that a part of this standstill in health may be due to increasing adverse drug reactions of all kinds, there is reason for concern. We may well be near the stage where the increase in drug consumption acts as a brake to real improvement in public health.

Clearly, advances in some fields are being made. But when one removes from this optimistic calculation the gains due to safer surgical treatment, advances in preventive care (many thousands will be spared illness and death from cancer of the lung from reduced smoking) and progress in achieving more adequate nutrition and sanitation, the argument claiming improvement in health by the increase in consumption of drugs becomes even more bare.

In psychiatry the battle rages regarding possible improvement in public health in this area. It is true that mental hospitals are being emptied, and for this all of us should sing praises – but not necessarily to the drug industry that has quickly claimed the credit. Part of the outflow from mental hospitals is due to a healthier public attitude to those with psychiatric handicaps and to more rigid criteria for admitting and retaining in hospital individuals who are merely 'peculiar'. Some part of the reduced mental hospital population is due to the near disappearance of the ravages of syphilis upon the nervous system. Syphilis itself, through preventive care and perhaps through the natural fluctuations of disease, was diminishing in occurrence, and by no means can all the credit for the reduction of the effect of syphilis on the nervous system be credited to drug treatment.

But parallel to this reduction in the population of mental hospitals has come a massive increase in the use of so-called mood controlling or psychoactive drugs. In the United Kingdom (1971) prescriptions for barbiturates reached twenty million per year, for phenylthiazine tranquillizers, six million; for amphetamines, five million; for non-barbiturate hypnotics, five million. Such amounts in the use of any class of drugs might be expected to show evidence of solid gain in public health. What is indeed evident is a vast increase in drug dependency, in adverse drug effects, in hospitalization for overdosage and in accidental and suicidal deaths.

And so, overall, where are the gains to justify the enormous expenditure of time, brains and money in industrial research and industrially sponsored an dpromoted mood-altering drugs? One must conclude that the greatest gain lies in the coffers of the drug industry.

Although many are unhappy about the powers held by the medical profession, there is little doubt that a licence to perform an operation on his fellow man should be granted only to a person with special education, subscribing to an ethical code and subject to continuing critical appraisal by his peers.

Whenever any group has exclusive rights for its own self-government a price must be paid. Within the profession of medicine the price is conformity to a group discipline and peer surveillance. It is this obedience through group discipline that has led the medical profession, in a curious way, to become the innocent junior partner of the industrial-medical complex.

Conformity is so much a part of the professional thing that it is hardly noticed by the individual professionals themselves. Most of medical education takes place in tightly knit conforming groups. In addition to this, peer-group review applies to many areas, most of which are relevant to the professional situation but some of which are not. Peer-group review demands practices which any doctor must know and observe. Treatments and procedures must have the general approval of one's peers. But in the same way many doctors accept the general ideas about society that are set by the conventional wisdom of their peer group. It is not by accident, but rather by training and conditioning, that most doctors are conservative and anti-radical in their views. Non-conformity in any area of thought is shunned and becomes subject to subtle covert sanctions, unofficial, but powerful enough to make most doctors fall in line and to shy away from the taint of being labelled a radical.

This leaning to concurrence has at times led to abuses. Because obedience is important in career decisions, the follower is more likely to achieve professional acceptance than the disturber. The more readily the junior follows the senior, the more smooth the path to professional success. Clinical training is by precept not by debate. 'Yes, sir' is the sound of ward rounds with the chief. In this context there indeed is no other way. The health and lives of patients are at stake. It would be risky to the point of disaster to permit students, interns or residents to try out on patients their own private ideas that are contrary to prevailing methods. But in this way obedience to conventional ideas is established and repeatedly reinforced.

Following graduation from the medical course, this pattern is continued. Professor Oswald Hall devoted a life-time to the study of the effects of career on the social attitudes of the medical practitioner. He has described career grouping of doctors, starting from an early apprenticeship system and evolving to the stage when the established senior doctor takes as an assistant or as a junior partner one who has a similar religious and social background to his own. The new boy must exhibit conventionally acceptable attitudes. In the larger English-speaking urban areas of the United States and Canada most hospitals are staffed either by Protestant doctors or by Roman Catholic doctors. In this way, in the larger centres, hospitals are either Catholic or Protestant orientated. More recently, with the increase in number of hospitals in larger centres, Jewish and Lutheran hospitals have developed as separate institutions in the medical-care area.

In the past there have been very few attempts to break this strict moulding process. Because the excursions of the pen are still free, these few attempts have centred in the 'heretical' writings of certain doctors. Many of these writings were not published, for the simple reason that most of the important medical journals are sponsored by particular medical societies, whose directors and editors were hardly inclined towards heresy. But there have been rare exceptions.

The most important of the journals that occasionally express other than conventional opinions are the *Lancet*, published in London, and the *New England Medical Journal*, published in Boston. Both are beacons jutting out of the tranquillity of conformity.

Founded by a heretic wealthy doctor (Thomas Wakley, 1795–

1862) the *Lancet* continues in the tradition – although somewhat subdued – set by this turbulent disturber of medical convention. Wakely graduated at a time when the apprentice system in the practice of medicine was riddled with nepotism. As a consequence, Wakely was thwarted in his desire to become a consulting surgeon in London. He led a campaign against the monopoly of surgical training and practice held by a hierarchy of members of the Royal College of Surgeons of London, to the point at which he was forcibly ejected from a meeting of the College. He initiated a campaign against the filthy disease-ridden quarters in which the sick poor were housed under the terms of the Poor Law Act of 1834. He published disclosures of contamination of food in general consumption. He publicly took the side of six trade-union members (still nearly an unheard action by a doctor) in the Tolpudle affair. In the medical profession the Wakleys are extremely rare.

Because of the modern insistent trend towards conformity, there is abiding reliance by members of the profession upon the attitudes of the leaders of the profession. The names of leaders of the profession appear in the pages of medical journals; therefore the pages of medical journals have a special charisma that few other journals enjoy. Even advertising pages share in this charisma. The very fact that products are advertised in the *British Medical Journal*, the *Journal of the American Medical Association*, the *Canadian Medical Journal*, and a number of other prestigious medical journals implies approval of those products by the Association that is sponsoring the particular journal. This message of apparent approval is reinforced by the fact that the journal carries the statement of firms manufacturing drugs and professional equipment, but no other general advertising for consumer goods, such as automobiles, washing machines and so on. In a curious way, therefore, both because of the disciplined habit of obedience to the guidance of leaders, and because no other advertising is permitted, the imprint of the drug manufacturer's advertisement obtains a subtle and persuasive impact on the professional reader. As a result of sophisticated insight by the advertiser, the trick in the advertising message is not only the message itself but the media. The reader need stop only long enough in the turning of advertising pages to read a patent name – preferably coloured and preferably in full-page glossy or, better still, double-page spread to be influenced. Practically every medical journal of any importance carries these attractive and enticing pages of advertising. Lorenz's ducklings have demonstrated the importance of 'imprinting', and wherever Lorenz leads the ducks obediently follow. The analogy of the medical profession following the leadership of the advertising pages by imprinting is fairly close.

It is difficult to over-estimate the importance to the journal of the revenue from advertising. The survival of the journal and the existence of the full-time administrative staff of the medical association depend on advertising. Few, if any, associations could maintain their considerable headquarters staff without this increment in revenue. Even the editor of the *New England Medical Journal*, a bright exception to the average run of professional journals, had this to say regarding advertising:

In 1968 the number of subscriptions of the journal ranged between one hundred and six thousand and one hundred and twelve thousand. The income from the subscriptions is roughly seven hundred and fifty thousand dollars. If it were to cover the entire cost of producing and distributing the journal, the income would have to be close to three million dollars. What makes up the difference of 2.2 million dollars or 75 per cent of the total? Advertising revenue. And more than three quarters of this or about 2 million comes from the promotion of drugs.*

The drug industry holds a tight, financial power of life or death over medical journals and over subordinated professional organizations. The control by industry over the medical part of the industrial-medical complex is further strengthened by other endeavours that have made doctors the unofficial sales staff of drug companies. In 1968 the United States Task Force on Prescription Drugs stated:

It is estimated that the major drug companies together now spend some three thousand dollars per physician annually to reach out to the nearly two hundred thousand physicians (United States) who

* *New England Medical Journal*, 4 Sept 1969, p. 257.

represent the target audience – those who will decide for which drug products their patients should pay.

By means of the industrial-medical complex the drug industry has achieved a unique market strength enjoyed by no other industry. Cars, soap, locomotives, compete with each other and, in addition, compete for the spendable dollar on the basis of price and quality. The drug industry is freed from this competitive struggle against other industries. For obvious reasons the prescription has a primary claim over all other expenditures.

But the most deplorable aspect of the industrial-medical complex is the erosion it has created in the doctor–patient relationship. Prior to the emergence of the industrial-medical complex it was the medical doctor who acted on behalf of the ill, especially the ill and poor. More than anyone else, the doctor entered their homes, saw their needs and recognized their ills. A bedside manner has become a joke, but it did at one time represent, among other things, an interested, conscientious, intimate and warm concern for the patient over and beyond the level of organic disease. The erosion of this close relationship may have begun with the employment of doctors by industry. Although originally intended to improve the lot of employees who became ill as a result of industrial processes, in many instances some doctors began to act in the interest of their employers, whenever a conflict of interest arose between the employer and the worker. He who pays the piper calls the tune. Some doctors employed and paid by industries fell under the control of the employer, and the traditional doctor–patient relationship could no longer exist under such circumstances.

The story of the asbestos processing industry, with its record of secrecy regarding the occurrence of asbestos-induced lung disease, has recently been told. The significant point in this unhappy story is that some doctors working for this industry ignored the evidence that an industrially induced health-hazard existed and, furthermore, resisted attempts by other doctors to bring the problem to light. In public hearings company doctors fudged efforts to legislate sanitation rules that could prove costly to industry, though intended to remove the hazard of asbestos-induced lung disease. It was the industrial-medical relationship that motivated doctors in the employ of the industry; not the patient–doctor relationship. It is noteworthy that it was workers' unions that took over the function, traditionally held by doctors, of championing the cause of the victims of this industrial hazard. It was also fortunate that a small group of independent medical researchers had the courage to pursue the researches in this field, notwithstanding industrial disapproval.

It takes courage to continue with a line of research that may take a direction running counter to the profit-maximization role of any particular industry. You might be cut off at the grant level. Your grant as an independent researcher doing your own thing may come from an apparently independent granting institution. But research institutes, even independent ones, must derive their funds from sources that have the funds to give. Financial support from some apparently independent research institutes may depend in part upon the largesse of firms, some of whom have a stake in limiting the spread of information that may lead to actions adverse to the financial interests of the firm.

Continuing Education – The Final Victory

In the evolution of the industrial-medical complex the first stage in the process of capturing the medical profession began with captive doctors working in the interests of their employers, not in the interests of their patients. From that stage the industrial-medical complex began actively to pursue and then to dominate the field of industrial drug production by capturing the entire profession.

The most decisive stage occurred when industrial forces assumed that most important area of influence in the practice of medicine – the field of continuing medical education.

Here a vacuum existed that was not created by industry. There was a curious absence of any tradition or institution within the medical educational establishments that could fill the information gap that occurs as soon as a doctor's formal education ends. This deficiency begins to operate the day that the neophyte doctor leaves the medical school and hospital environment and enters the field of medical practice.

The growth of medical information has been accelerating at an increasing pace since the beginning of this century. With this remarkable growth have come two effects. Firstly, the rapid obsolescence of what the doctor has been taught five, ten and certainly fifteen years ago. Secondly, the failure of professional organizations to do anything in any resolute or effective way to counteract the practising doctor's increasing ignorance about the spreading field of medical knowledge. It has been conservatively estimated that there is an almost complete turnover in medical information every ten years. Any practising doctor who does not read and digest a nearly impossible amount of research reports, in areas where he is likely to lack the basic knowledge for real comprehension, becomes even further removed from much that is essential for modern practice.

In more static fields of human knowledge – in classics, literature and in the areas of the arts and sciences of many universities – the 'sabbatical year' is a practice where, by a consensus of opinion, the decay of knowledge is restored by regular study-leave. A period of one year out of seven away from the routine duty imposed by the particular discipline is recommended for the repair and refreshment of the inventory of information and to give time for reflection.

This notion of a sabbatical year for the busy practitioner in the field of human health is practically unknown. In any activity where the effects of error or ignorance may well be catastrophic, and where the growth of information is astonishing, the practice of the sabbatical year is virtually unheard of.

The contrast seems remarkable. And yet professional organizations (representing voluntary associations of doctors such as the British, American and Canadian Medical Associations) have not in any forthright way encouraged their members to consider the idea of regular, formal study-leave. Nor have statutory medical societies (the ones that police professional standards) demanded, as a condition of retaining a licence to practice, the periodic return to study on the lines of a sabbatical.

The necessity for new information, ignored by professional

establishments, found a willing and eager provider in the drug industry. The industrial-medical complex became firmly established.

It was the drug industry that recognized the existence of this informational vacuum among practising physicians and has been working hard to fill it. While achieving success for its own goals, it provides at the same time a source of valuable information for the practitioner. The drug industry created a better informed but certainly more compliant doctor.

It would be unfair to be critical of the drug industry for its efforts to create a legitimate field of continuing education for the practising physician where none existed before. A good deal of the effort and expense by drug firms has a distinct educational value obtainable no other way. Seminars, conferences, meetings and much printed educational material, some of it of high quality, are sponsored and paid for by drug firms.* Many drug firms have established a highly organized educational branch. A reverse-charge telephone call over any distance is encouraged and accepted by firms from any practising physician. Full information is given by most drug manufacturing firms in an impartial way. Information brochures and pamphlets are available free. These contain up-to-date data and are profusely illustrated and explicit. Any doctor who wishes may make use of the educational material available from drug firms upon request and, providing he has the time and inclination to do so in the midst of a heavy practice, has access to a valuable source of continuing education.

Regrettably, it is not this area of industrially provided first-class continuing medical education that the average doctor uses. He receives, unsolicited, the second-level stuff. It is ubiquitous, frequent and almost constantly at his side, on his hospital rounds and in his consulting rooms, brought by the post or by the company representative. And he reads the advertisements attractively designed to be arresting to anyone leafing through the pages of the medical journal. This second-level flow makes up the greatest volume of informational material to the practising doctor. It is the sole source of information for far too many. The volume of this form of directed propaganda flow is enough to ensure

---

* The Ciba Company (based in Switzerland) is an example of the best in this area.

financial success for most new patent-name products, providing they are heavily detailed and aggressively advertised. The failures are few. They are incurred mostly by small, independent manufacturers, who lack the financial resources to launch an advertising promotional campaign where expense is no deterrent.

The top-level information – the material provided by the drug company for those who voluntarily seek it, the reliable data produced through a direct query by telephone, by seminars, by conferences, and so on – properly creates the image of an ethical firm. This image is so securely imprinted on the prescribing physician's mind that the second-level propaganda material is accepted without question as part of the total stream. It is a formula that works. It works well enough for the hand that writes the prescription to have been conditioned by the drug industry to write at the dictation of the firm. The interest of the patient has become compromised and subordinated. The doctor–patient relationship has become eroded and the financial interest of the firm now stands between patient and doctor. The industrial-medical complex has replaced the traditional doctor–patient relationship in the important decision for medication.

This situation has developed without villains. The drug industry has done what it must. In line with business ethos it has played its role for profit maximization. For the practising doctor, industry has filled a gap in the area of continuing education that, in view of the rapid pace of research, simply had to be filled. As soon as the fledgling doctor steps out of the period of formal education at medical school and hospitals, the drug industry continues his education for the remainder of his active professional life. The transition from university-orientated professional education to industry-orientated continuing education is a smooth one, and hardly commented upon in the professional journals, themselves depending for survival upon the industry. Conformity is so pervasive in the profession that this transition from one kind of education to another is accepted in a mindless, unquestioning way by nearly all doctors. Those doctors who complain are labelled as rebels or, worse, as radicals. Because of the structure of the profession, few doctors can withstand this kind of criticism.

Thus the goal of rational prescribing – the right drug for the right patient at the right time for the right price – remains an unrealized ideal in professional circles. Instead, the doctor becomes a cog in the predictable progression of engineered events that lead to assured sales and profits for the firm.

Harold Geneen, the wizard chief of the multinational conglomerate, International Telephone and Telegraph Co., has carried the industrial ethos of profit maximization to a functioning level from his high command. 'I want no surprises,' says Harold. Even in the assembly of corporations under Harold's command, he demands the ultimate in the field of accountancy. Every move must be carefully planned, perfectly executed, and finally lead always to the predictable bull's eye, the predetermined goal, without exception, without 'surprise'. For the bureaucrat in the drug industry the medical profession is an important and integral part of a smooth operation that starts with research and ends in the prescription. It is an operation that is designed to present no surprises and to surmount all obstructions to the predictable target of sales set by the marketing branch of the drug manufacturer. The industrial-medical complex is alive and well and assures the success of any drug-manufacturing firm that belongs to this cosy club of industrial giants.

The patient is excluded from this complex. He has neither knowledge nor choice. The patient can do nothing other than rely on the knowledge and choice of his doctor. He has only one function in this complex. He must in one way or another pay the price, whatever it may be.

The Bureaucratic Glue

The acquisition of overwhelming power for the drug industry within the health system arose from the change that occurred from owner-directed to bureaucratic-directed status. As long as owners directed and represented the dominant power within the system, the power of the drug companies was fragmented by competition. When, by mergers, the multinational megacorporation arose in the drug industry, bureaucratic control became absolute and cohesive, instead of fragmented and competitive.

Along with this a subtle but notable change took place in the meaning and significance of that banner of the corporate state: profit maximization. No longer did profit maximization have as its end point more money jingling in the owner's pocket. The owner now becomes a faceless mass of shareholders. The power adjustments were caused by this change. When the owner becomes thousands of shareholders, they can individually and even collectively exert little or no control on day-to-day decision-making.

Bureaucracies do not differ significantly, be they the bureaucracy of the White House, the Kremlin, the headquarters of the Roche Corporation in Zürich or the bureaucracy of the medical profession. In all these examples, the bureaucrat, irrespective of political or ideological stripe, is obliged to conform not to his private beliefs but to the fundamental rules that guide the bureaucracy. He must forfeit his own thoughts and private opinions to the imperatives that prevail within the system. He is obliged to strengthen and extend the influence of 'reach' of the organization. Personal freedom or real freedom of choice is beyond his reckoning. In this way the modern industrial bureaucrat does not differ in any essential, whether he resides in Moscow or London or New York or Zürich. Nor does he differ in any essential, whether he is in government, industry or a major professional association.

Thus, the acquisition of dominance in the health system by the industrial bureaucracy of the drug industry and the consequent subordination of the medical profession were accomplished smoothly by the same kinds of individuals within each bureaucracy. It is not by plot but by natural process that a President of the Pharmaceutical Manufacturing Association of Canada was an ex-president of the Canadian Medical Association. Nor is it surprising that two former Presidents of the American Medical Association served terms as First Officers to the Pharmaceutical Manufacturers' Association of the United States. At that level bureaucrats are interchangeable.

Along with a smooth power shift, the drug industry diverted a significant portion of its cash flow into the satellite professional bureaucracies, their journals and conventions. The effect of these

inputs has been to tie the bureaucracy of the medical profession
to a dominating drug industry in a tight and warm embrace – an
embrace so tight and warm that any attempt to separate it brings
out loud cries of pain from both the drug and the professional
bureaucracies.

Because doctors as a group are disciplined and accustomed to
accept the views of their leaders in political and economic matters,
there is rarely, if ever, any inclination to question the leadership
of the profession, even when the official pronouncements from
the medical bureaucracy closely echo drug-industry aims. At
government hearings and inquiries into the drug industry, statements from the bureaucracy of the medical profession cannot be
distinguished from statements by the industrial bureaucracy.
They are cut from the same cloth.

Choice – Who Has It?

Of three elements in this play for power within the health system
– doctors, patients, and industry – who has real freedom of
choice? Who among these three can significantly alter the flow of
influence?

We can forthwith dismiss the patient from any decision-
making area. The patient never did have, nor can he ever have,
real freedom of choice towards determining therapy. As an individual he may at his own risk exercise veto-power over treatment,
but that is not the same as freedom to select a particular drug or
a particular treatment. Traditionally, the decision-making power
to select drug or treatment rests with the doctor. That indeed is
the sole reason for the existence of the medical profession. By
consulting a doctor, the patient relinquishes his freedom of choice
over treatment and places his trust in a professional choice
exercised by his doctor. Consulting a doctor without this tacit
transfer of trust is meaningless.

Occasionally patients shop around to different doctors, with
the aim of discovering the various forms of treatment that may
be offered for the same disease. In this instance the patient makes
the choice among the varieties. This is wasteful and foolish, if

only for the reason that finally, when choice among the various treatments is made by the patient, it is a choice based upon a combination of ignorance and upon extraneous factors, such as good looks, attractive consulting room, social status, etcetera, of the doctor. One's health is too precious to be dependent upon the vagaries of such haphazard selection.

The patient's freedom of choice is virtually non-existent. It is exercised for him by the medical profession. Theoretically the doctor alone, on the basis of professional integrity, knowledge and skill, decides the prescription. But does the doctor, alone or with the help of his peers, really decide upon the specific drug?

Enough has been spent by the drug industry upon the medical profession to dilute seriously real freedom of choice that in theory is exercised by the doctor in the writing of his prescription. In very many instances he writes what the drug industry has conditioned him to write. The real situation as it affects the individual doctor is painfully ambivalent.

He may rigorously pursue professional integrity, ignore the importuning of the industry, ignore the samples, the advertisements in his journals, ignore the glossy stuff the postman brings, ignore the efforts of the company representatives – not easy because the human factor enters – and make up his own mind, based upon his own reading and on his own self-conducted, continuing education. This is difficult but not impossible.

But, for most, hurry skews the choice to the easier one of accepting what the industry by its massive promotion wants the doctor to write.

But, unlike the patient, who has no freedom of choice whatever, and unlike the industrial bureaucrat, whose actions are determined by imperatives, the individual doctor still has freedom of choice.

Unlike the bureaucrat, the doctor is a committed professional. The industrial bureaucrat, upon entering the system, must accept it and defer to the imperatives upon which the system operates. He cannot wreck the firm by acting against its interests; he can only comply or else depart. Within the system, for so long as he remains, he has no meaningful freedom of choice. The doctor on the other hand is consulted primarily because he has freedom of choice. That is the basis, the very soul of a true profession. A professional differs from a craftsman, from an executive, from an employee, from a technician, from a bureaucrat, in just this very essential respect. He exercises true freedom of choice on behalf of his client. If he does not, his behaviour is aberrant, unprofessional, and he renders a disservice to his patient.

Time is the limiting factor – the cause of hurry. Lack of it harries the doctor into shortcuts in professional conduct. For what reasons has doctors' time become such an important limiting and compromising element? After all, there are more and more doctors for the same number of people in developed countries. In some countries, for example Canada, there is worry that perhaps too many doctors are in practice. A few years ago in developed countries the accepted optimal distribution was one doctor for one thousand people, later reduced to one doctor for six hundred people. In Canada the level is one doctor for about five hundred and fifty people. It is not only costs that escalate with too many doctors.

If, as the apologists for the drug industry would have us believe, the health of people is vastly increased because of the boon of drugs available in the developed society, why should there be such a surge of patients requiring more and more doctors? If it is true, as claimed by the spokesmen of the drug industry, that 'The improved health of the Canadian people as a result of the modern therapeutic revolution represents a significant contribution to the economy of the entire nation'* – why more and more patients in Canada? Why are more and more doctors required? Why are costs escalating to an alarming degree? Why are the numbers of those taking time off work due to illness climbing, and why are doctors' waiting rooms bursting? Where is the evidence that 'the modern therapeutic revolution' is creating a significant contribution to the economy of the nation?

Are we involved in a controlled dance in a vicious cycle? Does the limit of time imposed by too many patients and by hurry

---

* *The Pharmaceutical Manufacturing Industry*, Pharmaceutical Manufacturers' Association of Canada (60 of the largest manufacturers comprising British, Canadian, French, German, Swedish, Swiss and United States Companies), 1973, p. 16.

force doctors to prescribe more and more industrially inspired drugs, creating more and more adverse drug effects and more and more drug dependency, and finally driving more and more people to doctors?

Another factor crowds the time of the busy practitioner: certificates. The more patients a doctor has, the more he is certain to have irresistible demands on his time to return various questionnaires and certificates to government bureaucracies and agencies, to insurance companies, to legal firms, to adoption agencies, and to pension boards. Some of these, by the sheer volume of detailed questions, are formidable documents, requiring re-examination of the patient and time-consuming searches of hospital records and the files of other doctors. Even those that have two or three lines of apparently simple questions may require a searching review of patients' files. These all take time. Little is left for study or thought or reflection.

Yet, in spite of all these constraints on his time, the doctor still remains the only one in the triumvirate of industry, patient and doctor, who can exercise freedom of choice about which drugs are prescribed. Despite the medical bureaucracy, the professional integrity of the individual doctor demands the exercise of this freedom on behalf of his patient.

11 Is There a Government Around?

In this irresistible drive by industry – with the compliant co-operation of the profession – towards more and more pills – is there any effective action that governments can take to stem the growing flood?

The outlook is not promising. Government bureaucracies share the imperatives of all other bureaucracies to conform to a rigid frame of reference. The limits are set, partly by policy and partly by the rigidities inherent in any governmental bureaucratic system. Policy set by democratic action is broad, bland and well meaning. Policy in health matters is, like motherhood, difficult to attack. It aims for the 'better'. Better drugs could well mean more and more drugs – and it is not the aim of government to stop the drive of 'progress'. Governments as a matter of basic policy must encourage the goal of industrial growth. Private enterprise in the drug manufacturing industry, as in all industrial endeavour, is supported by government and ought not to be discouraged by heavy-handed government restraint or control.

At best, government intervention in the control of the drug industry represents a trade-off – a compromise between divergent aims within the government bureaucracy itself. Governments aim for an increasing gross national product, full employment, encouragement for industrial goals, and growing tax revenues as a result of bustling industrial activity. Government agrees with industry that mass consumption and a higher standard of living are equally adorable twins. And if mass consumption has produced the post-war prosperity of the western countries since the Second World War, Governments are not about to tamper with a rising economy. Not only is the economy of mass production helpful, it is also accepted as the proven standard in governmental circles, and it is not to be questioned by such apparently radical notions as 'limits of growth'. The bureaucracy of government, like all bureaucracies, is impersonal and depends upon unquestioned standards and not upon individual evaluations or way-out beliefs. And since no easy solution exists in government areas, the aim of mass consumption of drugs is the same as mass consumption of any other commodity. The concept of 'limits of growth' has a long way to go before it reaches the halls of government – even with drug consumption.

Indeed, for much the same reasons, the problem of mass consumption of drugs is neither a matter of public awareness nor a subject for public debate. The public has faith in all the responsible areas: the drug industry, the government, the medical and pharmaceutical professions. In a matter so technical, so full of big words, scientific concepts, and jargon, public debate does not take place.

Furthermore, the increasing movement of industry towards a multinational network has discouraged government intervention in the few areas where control has been attempted. Intervention into thalidomide was too little and too late. With the exception of the Government of the United States, it was not governments that stopped the sale of thalidomide. And even in the case of the United States Government, it was less the action of government than the refusal of a single tough-minded employee, Dr Kelsey, who refused to pass on the request for approval to higher authorities. Elsewhere, it was industry itself, faced with a mountain of evidence and a tidal wave of law suits, that stopped the sales.

But, assuming the will, can governments influence the multinationals in any way?

The record does not allow one to make an optimistic prediction. Political scientists have warned of threats to the democratic system by the growing dominance of multinationals over sovereign governments. Anthony Sampson * in his exposure of International Telephone and Telegraph Co. has tried to show that clandestine movements by a multinational can give it licence that extends beyond the laws of any country and may bend and influence key figures in some governments. The British Govern-

* Sampson A., *The Sovereign State*, Hodder & Stoughton, London, 1973.

ment's confrontations with Roche were hardly a clear victory of government over multinational.

Although the situation has improved slowly – too slowly in most countries – the protective mantle of government has not yet protected the public's interest, concerning the introduction of drugs that are later proven to be a detriment to public health. The reason for this ambiguous response by government is not difficult to find.

Democracy is at its best in a pluralist society, when many different groups and bodies exert their influence on government. The government, as fairly as it can in the general public interest, then decides on its action – often a compromise between conflicting interests. Business, labour, professions, consumers, and minority groups of all sorts give expression to the diverse interests that are bound to be present in any evolved society. These interests express their views and their pressures legally and without fear of persecution. Furthermore, the instruments of communication, the press, radio and public address are presumed to present each side fairly and free from repression or bias. It is inevitable that such differing groups will clash and contend with one another and that the determination of public policy must depend on something less than unanimous consent. But the predominance of the objectives of one group alone, without concessions being made to opposing views, creates unfair imbalances that become intolerable.

So the interests of industrial groups are balanced by the contentions of labour and sometimes by vocal consumer groups. The common denominator, theoretically at least, remains the general public good.

Such a state can contain and protect many religions, many philosophies, many ethnic groups, many different people, expressing ideas in different ways. It is marked by a wide dispersion of power and by the existence of many centres for influencing government decisions. In such a democratic system the groups have distinctive characteristics. They are independent of each other, autonomous, self-supporting, and strong enough to exert pressure from outside and to maintain their integrity when the struggle is severe. Moreover, on the contemporary scene, these groups are usually specialized: drug manufacturers, unions involved in the drug industry, professional groups of various kinds and so on. This kind of confrontation between countervailing forces is seen to be in the public interest in a market economy.

But let us stop a minute in this idealistic jaunt. Where is the countervailing force to the immense power of the multinational drug companies? The natural one would be a claque of the ill. But the ill are too old, too young, too poor, too inarticulate, too disabled or debilitated and, furthermore, too transient in existence to become any kind of demonstrable force. In contrast the representatives of the drug companies, with their sophisticated public-relations experts, accountants and lawyers, walk proudly in the corridors of power. They are never confronted by a special group representing the ill. In fact, there is no countervailing force to the power of the drug companies.

In some countries the ill are more exposed to the economic drive of the drug companies than in others. Thus the United States Task Force on Prescription Drugs (1968) described the group of elderly ill in the United States as follows:

For many elderly people, illness serves as a major cause of their poverty by reducing their incomes while poverty serves as a major contributory cause of illness by making it impossible for them to obtain adequate health care.

But their inordinate health needs, their high health care costs in general and high drug costs in particular, and their limited financial resources combine to create a serious and sometimes a devastating medical and economic problem far out of proportion to their numbers.

Yet it is not only the totally impoverished or the totally incapacitated who are in a precarious position. There are many elderly men and women who have some income and some savings – who may even have sufficient Medicare or other insurance to protect them against the bulk of hospital and medical costs of a brief illness – but who cannot pay for out-of-hospital drugs and other costs of long-continuing chronic illness without seeing their financial assets eroded or totally dissipated. . .

Thus the elderly with limited income, limited savings and minimal protection from health insurance and other sources are obliged to face the burdens of drug costs which are far heavier on a per capita basis than those which weigh on their fellow citizens who in most cases are younger, healthier, and wealthier. . .

We find, therefore, that the requirements for appropriate prescription drug therapy by the elderly are very great – far greater in fact than those of any other group, and that many elderly men and women are now unable to meet these needs with their limited incomes, savings or present insurance coverage. Their inability to afford the drugs they require may well be reflected in needless sickness and disability, unemployment, and costly hospitalization which could have been prevented by adequate out-of-hospital treatment.

With steadily increasing prescription expenditures this problem is destined to become increasingly serious.

What kind of a pressure group can these unfortunates produce? They do not parade, they chant no slogans, carry no banners, present no briefs. They have no organization and exert no pressure. No more quiet or submissive group exists. In our democratic society is it any wonder that there is a powerful, sophisticated, well-organized group on one side, exerting influence upon the important government bureaux that exist to control the distribution of drugs, and rarely a peep from any opposing group?

The doctor, as the traditional spokesman for the ill, is capable of exerting his influence and the power of his associations on the patient's behalf in decisions regarding the manufacture of drugs. This has not happened. Because the power of the multinational drug industry is alert, active and forceful, one might have expected that the medical profession and its associations would have presented an opposing power on behalf of the ill. Sadly this is not so. Almost every time that questions are raised and statements made, the bureaucrats of organized medicine side with the bureaucrats of the multinational drug industry. This relationship is warm and close while the interests of the ill are subordinated.

This must change. To continue to move submissively along the road paved by the industrial-medical complex is to concentrate upon profits for the few and to increase the supply of stupefying drugs for the many.

There is a way out. There is a possibility of real change that depends not on the industry, not on governments, not on medical associations, but entirely and solely on the action of individual doctors – the men at the front line of professional activity.

12   The Coming Struggle for the Prescription Pad

The natural place for the doctor is at the side of the patient. In spite of all the criticism of the modern doctor he is still the only one left in our society with whom one can have an intimate, confidential, face to face meeting. In a society where bigness holds sway; where supermarkets replace the grocer; where furniture emporia replace the cabinet maker; where the assembly line has displaced the shoemaker, the baker, the candlestick maker; where charity is no longer a personal thing but the writing of a cheque to an appeal committee – the doctor is still there to be called and be met in an atmosphere where only the patient counts.

Thus there are good reasons for individual doctors to thrust themselves into the struggle for rational prescribing. They are physically closest to the patient and, in spirit and dedication, to his welfare. Furthermore, they can hit the multinational drug companies where it will hurt and be effective – in the cash box.

Who else but the individual doctor, true to his Hippocratic oath, can support the ill in their unequal contest with an aggressive, profit-motivated, multinational industry? If enough are willing, they may be a powerful enough force to change the course of the multinationals. This is something that the medical associations have had no wish to do and governments have failed to do. Individual doctors have only to say NO loudly and clearly.

Within a true profession the individual member must place the highest value upon the statement of a professional code – a code that is universal and for all time. Not even the leaders of professional associations may alter this historic code. When the leaders of the profession in Nazi Germany changed the rules, to make it permissible to force human experiments of the most brutal kind on the inmates of the concentration camps, it became mandatory for individual doctors to disobey their leaders –

no matter what the consequence of this disobedience. The obedience that a doctor owes to his peer group is always subordinate
to his over-riding obligation to refuse any practice that offends
the code of the profession or the moral conscience of the individual doctor.

This belief in the importance of the negative response was best
stated by Jean-Paul Sartre, who in effect said: 'The essential
freedom, the ultimate and final freedom that cannot be taken
from man, is to say NO.' To disobey, in accordance with one's
professional code and in accordance with the dictates of one's
own moral conscience, is the highest assertion of professional
integrity. The time has come for the individual doctor to be the
spearhead of the revolt that is necessary to break apart the
industrial-medical complex and to direct the profession to its
proper task: supporting the interests of the ill. In this kind of
revolt doctors have nothing to lose but their samples. They may
regain the moral dignity of the profession. They will certainly
preserve their own.

What can individual doctors do? A lot, and easily, and without having to organize.

1. As individuals, they can stop using brand names in prescribing. This single step by itself may save millions to patients
and to taxpayers and stop the rush of the drug industry to the
new brand – no better but more costly. It can stop engineered
market obsolescence and spurious research in the development of
new products, no better than the old but more profitable. It can
reduce dramatically the effects of adverse reactions of new drugs,
reactions sometimes not recognized but nevertheless accounting
for thousands of patients in hospitals, many deaths and incalculable social costs. Evidence before the American Senate Sub-
committee on Health (18 December 1973) was to the effect that
'the most conservative estimate of FDA (Food and Drug Administration) is that there are about one hundred Americans dying
every day because of adverse drug reactions. Add to this an estimated three billion dollars per year for institutional care due to
adverse drug reactions.'

These figures, applying to one country, may be difficult to
substantiate, but there is no doubt that world-wide figures are

much greater. While the ignoring of trade names will not completely stop this toll of adverse reactions, it would discourage the industry from introducing and promoting drugs with new brand names merely in order to stimulate sales.

2. They can refuse to accept medical journals that carry drug advertising. Hopefully this will demolish a substantial percentage of the over-large number of professional journals. It will vastly improve the quality of those that survive. One would shed bitter tears if two of the best journals in the English language (the *Lancet* and the *New England Medical Journal*) went under, but I doubt very much that they would. Most doctors (especially the doctors in revolt) would pay an additional subscription cost to keep the few quality journals alive without advertisements. Freed of the corrupting influence of drug advertising, journal editors could be more selective in their choice, more trenchant in their criticism. New drugs would be introduced not as fanfare advertisements but as editorial announcements, with prominent coverage in bold type of the possible adverse effects, in addition to a frank opinion of the value of the new drug in comparison with the old and also with the price of the new in comparison with the old.

3. The responsibility of continuing medical education should be removed from the too-willing shoulders of the drug companies. Medical conventions can be held without the corridors and halls being cluttered with drug displays. If the association heads responsible for holding the conventions continue in this practice of commercial displays, then the doctors in revolt should refuse to attend and should state their refusals to their elected officers. Instead of the industrial drug displays, with their samples and other goodies, booths supervised by university- or teaching-hospital staffs could be installed at each convention. At these booths a personal chat for five minutes with a knowledgeable expert on the treatment of a particular disease would do much good, and infinitely less harm than hours of intensive brain washing by the propaganda machine of the industry.

Universities, with support by fees from doctors and by government grants, can employ their own representatives to detail individual doctors on drugs, in much the same way that industrial representatives now do, but without the industry-directed bias. These university representatives (especially trained pharmacists) could keep individual doctors informed of new developments in the drug field by annual or semi-annual visits. In particular, they could give, and get, reports of adverse reactions to known and otherwise useful drugs. Serious defects in newer drugs could be discovered earlier than was the case with thalidomide. The gain could have been thousands of limbs.

4. The doctors in revolt should all, every single one of them, subscribe to the *Medical Letter* (United States) and to the *Prescribers Journal* (United Kingdom). There are today no clearer more conscientiously truthful statements regarding new drugs appearing on the market. Needless to say these magazines carry no advertising and rely entirely on the support of the subscribers. Furthermore, these journals have the honesty to change their opinions in the light of new facts as they become evident.

5. There is one other thing revolting doctors can voluntarily do. They can treat their own urge to prescription writing as they treat compulsive eating in their obese patients : trim off the fat. Doctors write too many prescriptions; some far too many. This tendency, more than any other, has placed doctors under the control of the drug industry. Where the indication for specific medication is clear, there is no doubt as to what should be written, hopefully avoiding the trade name. But it is in that large proportion of cases when the doctor has really not the foggiest idea what to prescribe that he automatically (even mindlessly) writes something to indicate that the session is over.

The patient can learn other symbols indicating that the interview is over. The doctor at this crucial moment (instead of reaching for the pad) may rise to his feet, extend a hand, say he is delighted that there is nothing seriously wrong and that he would be happy to see the patient again if the trouble recurs, and that there is reasonable certainty that the illness will disappear by itself. The doctor will be awkward about this at first and the patient, if still apprehensive, will say : 'Are you not going to give me some medicine?' The answer should be a firm 'No'. One could reply, 'I would like to see what medications you already have in your medicine cabinet. Some of them might be useful and I will have a better idea of what else may be required. Be sure to bring all your medications, whether you are now using them or not, the next time you come.' One or two things will happen: the patient may not return saying, 'that doctor is daft, he didn't give me any medicine' and perhaps go off to another doctor who may hopefully be another in revolt, or the patient may indeed come with a bag full of medicines, dating back from goodness knows when. The doctor should be prepared for a shock. He may be amazed to learn that the patient is already taking two or three different-trade-name equivalents of the drug that he was intending to prescribe. These may well have accounted for the symptoms. At any rate the opportunity for boldness now exists. In the interest of the patient and in the interest of public health any repetitive or unused drugs should be discarded in the waste-paper basket. The home will suddenly become a safer and healthier place. Even the life of a child may be spared. If only a 10 per cent decrease in prescribing takes place in this way, a blow will have been struck for mankind. The opportunity of saying 'No', kindly though firmly, is a moment of professional integrity, a declaration of professional freedom and a put-down to the industrial-medical complex.

6. There is one area where compulsion may be justified and should be supported by the profession. All advertising of drugs in the public media should be stopped – the press, magazines, radio and T.V. No one except the media will suffer. Many thousands will be spared the countless hours of boredom at the inane stupidities and sheer lies these advertisements exhibit. There is literally nothing that can be said honestly in their favour. For the ignorant, the innocent, or individuals who believe everything, they constitute a real menace, because in their ludicrous way they appear convincing. What could be more dramatic than seeing a stuffed nose become unstuffed before your very eyes; a hacking cough suddenly disappear; a pill swallowed and zoom, it's right up there, inside your head, doing its stuff; bowels moving confidently; sleep quietly taking place instead of tossing and turning; relaxed determination replacing hand wringing; anguish ending; pain disappearing immediately; and the queasy, heaving stomach becoming tranquil.

If this kind of pernicious nonsense were stopped, there is reason to believe that much of the mindless adult pill-popping would be reduced and small children would have a healthier environment.

There is encouraging evidence that the restriction of tobacco advertising has already reduced the number of smokers. As a result, thousands will be spared the misery and death of lung cancer. A similar effect can be expected from a restriction of all drug advertising. If you like you may include alcohol in the advertising ban without in the least spoiling anyone's enjoyment of a convivial drink and without in the least reducing the quality of life.

All but the last of the above measures can be effected without legislation and without requiring the cooperation of the officers of professional associations. If enough individual doctors revolt in this non-violent manner, the industrial-medical complex will wither. The industry may be induced to re-examine the direction of its research and there may be less aggressive promotion of new pills. There may be a reduction in profits; there will certainly be a reduction in the social costs of adverse drug reaction along with a reduction in the growing amount of the illness caused by drugs. And finally the prescription pad may be wrested from the control of the drug industry back to where it belongs – under the control of the individual doctor. The day of rational prescribing may yet arrive.

More about Penguins and Pelicans

Penguinews, which appears every month, contains details of all the new books issued by Penguins as they are published. From time to time it is supplemented by *Penguins in Print*, which is a complete list of all titles available. (There are some five thousand of these.)

A specimen copy of *Penguinews* will be sent to you free on request. For a year's issues (including the complete lists) please send 36p if you live in the United Kingdom, or 60p if you live elsewhere. Just write to Dept EP, Penguin Books Ltd, Harmondsworth, Middlesex, enclosing a cheque or postal order, and your name will be added to the mailing list.

In the U.S.A.: For a complete list of books available from Penguin in the United States write to Dept CS, Penguin Books Inc., 7110 Ambassador Road, Baltimore, Maryland 21211.

In Canada: For a complete list of books available from Penguin in Canada write to Penguin Books Canada Ltd, 41 Steelcase Road, Markham, Ontario L3R 1B4.

Published in Pelicans

Studies in Social Pathology

Alcoholism *Neil Kessel and Harry Walton*
'Alcoholism is a disease, and commonly a disease of the mind, of the whole personality rather than of the body; the disease can be treated and cured ... This is the message of an impressive little book' – *Guardian*

Dying *John Hinton*
The rational and irrational emotions associated with death are discussed in this original study by a psychiatrist who has long been concerned with patients suffering from incurable illnesses.

The Psychotic *Andrew Crowcroft*
Dr Crowcroft's book, with its clear outline of social and physical treatments available today, is concerned with psychosis – true madness – in a way which has not previously been attempted in a popular edition.

Sexual Deviation *Anthony Storr*
This book is a brief account of the common types of sexual behaviour which are generally considered perverse or deviant, together with explanations of their origins.

Suicide and Attempted Suicide *Erwin Stengel*
Professor Stengel's authority and, in particular, his research on attempted suicide, make this a book of real importance. The author draws throughout on a wealth of international research into the incidence, methods, and social and personal dynamics of suicidal acts.

Venereal Diseases *R. S. Morton*
Here a specialist makes a full study both of the personal and social aspects of syphilis, gonorrhea, and other diseases associated with sex.

Andrew Weil

The Natural Mind

The Natural Mind is one of the most original and thoughtful statements about drugs since Huxley's *Doors of Perception*.

Andrew Weil is a qualified doctor and his views are based on medical research as well as personal experience. In his opinion the use of drugs may be as natural as children spinning to 'make the world go round' – as harmless, in some cases, as skin-diving . . . more harmless, certainly, than alcohol.

Drugs, he believes, offer a way, and probably not the best, of achieving a change of consciousness – something man has always needed. Only our attitude to them creates a 'problem'.

To those who are impatient with the limitations of materialistic thinking this book is bound to appeal. For, beyond the minor questions of drugs, it points invitingly to the great untapped resources of the human mind.

Not for sale in the U.S.A. or Canada

Paul Vaughan

The Pill on Trial

No drug in the history of medicine has caused so much controversy as the contraceptive pill. Does it solve the population problem, neatly, safely and humanely? Or has science been too clever and is there an unknown risk attached?

In any case the pill is part of the social revolution of our times: it gives women, for the first time in history, the same sexual freedom as men and compels us to think again about accepted ideas on sex and marriage.

In this book – specially revised and brought up to date for this Pelican edition – a medical journalist of distinction examines the facts behind the headlines, telling the remarkable story of how the pill came to be discovered and reviewing in detail the evidence on its safety. Paul Vaughan discusses too the pill's effects on sexual customs and on the growth of world population.

'An excellent piece of reporting, accurate . . . sober but amusingly written, and admirably detached' – *Nature*

'Well told . . . employs a first-class scientific journalist's skill to bring the story alive' – *Listener*

Not for sae in the U.S.A.

Peter Laurie

Drugs
Medical, Psychological and Social Facts

Second Edition

What are the known facts about the 'dangerous' drugs? What actual harm, mental or physical, do they cause? Which of them are addictive, and how many addicts are there?

Peter Laurie has talked with doctors, policemen, addicts, and others intimately involved with this problem. He has tried some of the drugs for himself and closely studied the medical literature (including little-known reports of American research). The result of his inquiries into the pharmacological uses and social effects of drugs today appears in this book.

Originally published as a Penguin Special which went through five printings, *Drugs* was the first objective study to offer all the major medical, psychological and social facts about the subject to a public which is too often fed with alarmist and sensational reports. For this second edition in Pelicans Peter Laurie has added fresh information and statistics concerning English users of drugs and noted changes in the law.

A Penguin Special

The Non-Medical Use of Drugs

Interim Report of the Canadian Government Commission of Inquiry

Here is a direct, clearly written, and very human survey of today's drug scene in all its aspects. The writers understand 'drug' to mean any sedative, stimulant, tranquillizing, hallucinogenic, or other psychotropic chemical – a definition that takes in alcohol and tobacco as well as more notorious substances like marijuana, hashish, LSD, heroin and 'speed'. Their report does much more than consider the drugs themselves – it examines in eye-opening detail every dimension of non-medical drug use and drug-related behaviour, including the religious and the sexual. In addition the book offers an in-depth view of one country's use of law as a response to the drug explosion.

Undertaken by the Canadian government, the research on which this book is based was never allowed to stray from the actual experiences of people who use drugs. In fact coffee houses and universities played a key role in the investigation. And among the six appendices is a special selection of letters from private citizens – some warmly in favour of wider legalization – others indignant in their expressions of grief and outrage.

When this volume appeared in Canada it created a sensation. Its recommendations, which are often surprising, will provoke as much discussion in other countries. For drugs, whether they bring delight to the senses or death to the body, are now a phenomenon that no one can ignore.

Not for sale in Canada

Thalidomide and the Power of the Drug Companies

Henning Sjöström and Robert Nilsson

Thalidomide ... was this just an innocent case of a tranquillizer turning out to have monstrous side-effects on children to be born? Or was something uglier at work in its destructive career?

A Swedish lawyer and a research chemist have pieced together, for this Penguin Special, the story of the companies that made and sold the drug.

They argue that thalidomide was known to be dangerous (for the damage it could do to the nervous system) when it was put on the market; that the threat represented to children in the womb was recognized for some time before it was withdrawn.

Recalling the legal battles which were fought around the drug in Western Europe, the U.S.A., Japan and Australia, the authors (one of whom actively advised the prosecution in some countries) do not hesitate to name the scientists working for the companies and quote from their evidence and memoranda. Their story strongly suggests that the mysteries of science may place too much power in the hands of those who are out for profits, and in their final chapter they propose ways of preventing the tragic case of thalidomide being repeated.

Not for sale in Scandinavia